Hester Lynch Piozzi

Glimpses of Italian Society in the Eighteenth Century

Hester Lynch Piozzi

Glimpses of Italian Society in the Eighteenth Century

ISBN/EAN: 9783744760997

Printed in Europe, USA, Canada, Australia, Japan

Cover: Foto ©ninafisch / pixelio.de

More available books at **www.hansebooks.com**

GLIMPSES
ITALIAN SOCIETY

IN THE EIGHTEENTH CENTURY

From the 'Journey in Italy' of
MRS. PIOZZI

WITH AN INTRODUCTION
BY THE
COUNTESS EVELYN MARTINENGO CESARESCO

NEW YORK
CHARLES SCRIBNER'S SONS
743-745 BROADWAY
1892

CONTENTS

CHAPTER	PAGE
INTRODUCTION	1
I. TURIN AND GENOA	42
II. MILAN	59
III. MANTUA, VERONA, AND PADUA	91
IV. VENICE	102
V. FERRARA AND BOLOGNA	139
VI. FLORENCE	150
VII. LUCCA, LEGHORN, BATHS OF PISA, SIENA	179
VIII. ROME	206
IX. NAPLES	215
X. ROME REVISITED	261
XI. RETURN TO MILAN	281
XII. LAGO MAGGIORE—RETURN TO VERONA	304

LIST OF ILLUSTRATIONS

	PAGE
PILGRIMS IN ST. PETER'S. AFTER DAVID ALLAN -	*Frontispiece*
MR. AND MRS. PIOZZI - - - - -	4
A LADY SPINNING. AFTER PIETRO LONGHI - -	84
VENICE: THE PIERA DEL BANDO. AFTER CANALETTO -	104
VENICE: THE ISLAND OF S. GIORGIO. AFTER GUARDI -	110
VENICE BY NIGHT. AFTER MORETTI - - -	128
A CARNIVAL SCENE. AFTER TIEPOLO - - -	132
A BARGE ON THE BRENTA. AFTER COSTA - -	136
ROME: THE PIAZZA DEL POPOLO. AFTER VASI - -	206
THE GROTTA DEL CANE. AFTER RAPHAEL MORGHEN -	234
CHRISTMAS EVE: CALABRIAN PEASANTS. AFTER DAVID ALLAN - - - - - - -	238
ANCIENT BATHS AT BAIÆ. AFTER RAPHAEL MORGHEN	252
A NEAPOLITAN DANCE. AFTER DAVID ALLAN - -	258
ROME: THE PIAZZA NAVONA. AFTER VASI - -	262
THE PONTINE MARSHES. AFTER RAPHAEL MORGHEN -	268
A HERMIT ON THE APPIAN WAY. AFTER DAVID ALLAN	274

GLIMPSES OF ITALIAN SOCIETY

IN THE

EIGHTEENTH CENTURY

INTRODUCTION

THE bulk of the writers of books of travel in the sixteenth and seventeenth centuries approached us less nearly in feeling than did the Roman youths of an earlier age, who carried their warmest enthusiasm to the land where they could tread on history. Italy, the Greece of the modern world, found them critical and left them cold. Rabelais, for instance, could not for the life of him see what there was to admire in Florence. Had the Elizabethan dramatists depended on such reports alone, it would be difficult to understand how they managed to absorb, as they did, the idea and atmosphere of the South. But England was flooded with Italian literature and full of Italians, who taught all the arts and amenities of civilization—in which way, rather than from travellers' tales, arose the enormous debt of English poetry to Italy.

In the eighteenth century the number of English travellers vastly increased, and still more the proportion of those who wrote books. It began to occur to everyone to take up his pen as soon as he set down his valise. Out of the mass of volumes thus produced, some have a permanent value, such as the writings of Addison, Brydone, Swinburne, Arthur Young, and, for musical matters, Dr. Burney. Meanwhile, Smollett and Samuel Sharpe went collecting the opposite of roses. Sharpe's book is wholly forgotten, together with Baretti's answer or refutation; Smollett's chapters of accidents are chiefly recollected for his comparison of the Pantheon to a cockpit with a hole atop. Only Goldsmith, who trudged on foot through part of Italy, as Tom Coryat had done a hundred and fifty years before, and who could have written the most interesting tour of all, did not write one. How much we should like to have his account of the peasant hosts who gave him bread or polenta in return for his flute-playing!

With a public ready to read any quantity of Italian descriptions and gossip, it was a foregone conclusion that so facile a writer as Mrs. Piozzi would not long withhold the results of her travels in Italy. She had several exceptional advantages for observing the ways of the people; to begin with, she was the wife of an Italian, and the fact of her sex was in itself fortunate, for women—as has been proved since by squadrons of lady-voyagers—are more observant of small things than men. She did not bring out her book in the usual form of letters, for she says it would have been a pure piece of hypocrisy, as her old acquaintances troubled her with very few tender inquiries during her absence. Poor woman! she went on her journey smarting under, though by no means crushed by, the solemn outburst, after her second marriage, of that sort of moral indignation which seeks to compensate by volubility for its lack of rational ground. It may be granted that a widow with grown-up daughters does not generally do the wisest thing imaginable when she renews the marriage tie, and in Italy, among the peasants, the step might lead to her receiving one evening a serenade of tin-kettles and saucepans. But the charivaris of polite society are more cruel, and, besides, the question of whether a widow of forty should or should not re-marry had nothing really to do with the acrimony with which Mrs. Thrale was treated by people, most of whom had strong reasons to be grateful to her. The cause of the attack lay in the childish caste prejudices of persons who were probably no better born than Piozzi; but, then, they were Britons, and they had never taught music, which, of course, proved their respectability. Such prejudices die hard; in this century an Italian who, like Piozzi, had made a substantial fortune by teaching music in England, had no end of difficulty in persuading a worthy English wine-merchant to become his father-in-law; the objections were expressly based on rank, which was amusing, because the music-teacher was of an illustrious Neapolitan family. He used to tell the story of his wooing with much gusto to his friends in Italy. Mrs. Piozzi was anxious that her residence abroad should prove not only an escape from the range of those 'poisoned arrows of private malignity' of which she speaks in her preface, but also a means of raising Piozzi in the eyes of the world by showing that he was cordially welcomed in his own country. On his side, he had an honourable desire that they should remain out of England till Mrs. Piozzi's debts were paid, which was soon accomplished, thanks to his good management.

In spite of spite, they set out in the best of spirits, provided with 'a magnificent carriage' full of tea and books—the latter had originally comprised a

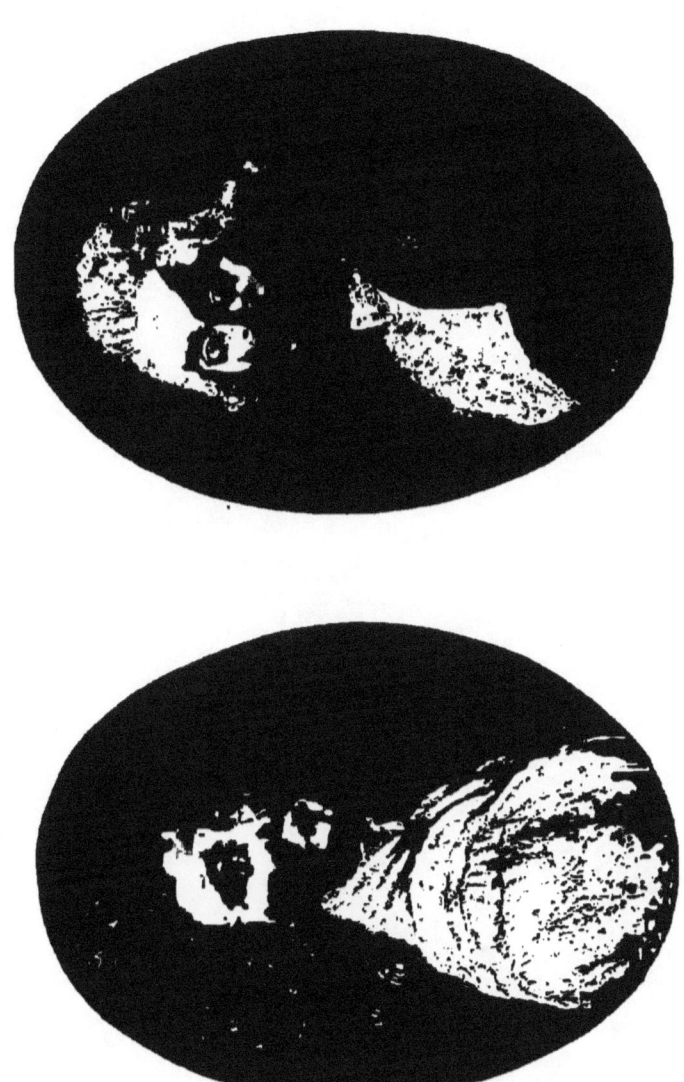

Mrs. Piozzi.   Signor Piozzi.

From Portraits in the possession of Signor Enrico Piozzi, of Brescia.

copy of Diodati's translation of the Bible, but this was omitted at the request of Piozzi, who advised his 'dear creature' to be content with the English version and to remember that she was travelling as the wife of a native and a papist. Much later than that, the possession of Diodati might have caused the trouble which Piozzi sensibly declined to encounter. With all her liveliness, Mrs. Piozzi had serious religious convictions and a definite attachment to her own Church; but she was willing that other folk should go to heaven by the road they preferred, and her hardest remark about the Roman faith was that she would never submit to call those Catholics who excluded from salvation every Christian sect save their own. She was fond of the society of courtly ecclesiastics, and the interior of convents had for her the kind of fascination which a cloistered life often exercises over rather worldly people. She had scarcely arrived at Calais on this journey, when she went to renew her acquaintance with the Dominican sisters in that town, and she was mortified at finding that they had completely forgotten not only their visitor, but also her eldest daughter, whom she had taken many years before to see them. She wondered how it was possible to forget so beautiful a child: a rather pathetic little note to have been written just then, when the daughter, who inherited all Mr. Thrale's sound but somewhat chilly qualities, was not treating her mother in the most amiable manner. Mrs. Piozzi consoled herself with the story of the dervish who contemplated the possibility of his forgetting even the splendour of the Great Mogul because he was always thinking of God; it was the same, she supposed, with nuns: 'No one is of importance to a nun, who is and ought to be employed in other speculations.' A reflection that shows a power of insight into orders of feeling different from her own, which no doubt had much to do with making Mrs. Piozzi easily popular among all sorts and conditions of men and, which is the harder, of women.

In Paris the travellers found the town mad for love of a new comedy, 'Le Mariage de Figaro,' the epoch-making play which, as Carlyle said, 'Spoke what all were feeling and longing to speak.' They were introduced to Goldoni, 'garrulous, good-humoured and gay,' who was held in high estimation by his countrymen in the French capital. At eighty-four the light-hearted old Venetian was busily engaged in writing his memoirs. Little did he foresee the deluge that was going to engulf him. He died of profound melancholy in 1792, the Revolution having robbed him of his means of sustenance; an end that reminds one of Auber's death during the Commune, when a common grave received the unidentified dust of the musical veteran who had added so much to the world's gaiety. It is a wise law of nature that butterflies should live but for a day. Mrs. Piozzi was anxious to have the opportunity of meeting Italians and of talking the language with strangers—which she did not find easy; and she derived much pleasure from the conversation of two or three well-known Milanese noblemen who were living in Paris. After three weeks agreeably spent, she and her husband left for Turin; her description of the route overflows with a passionate delight in the beauties of nature, of which she was a better judge than of the beauties of art, though she had an equal love for both. The remarks on descriptions of scenery in general are acute. 'One half despairs of communicating one's ideas as they are; for either well-chosen words do not present themselves, or being well-chosen they detain the reader and fix his mind on them instead of the things described.' The cattle grazing by the Yonne, whose banks were clothed with the royal purple of some wild flower, the expansive views of a productive country where vineyards covered the hills and the young wheat filled the valleys, the ceaseless variety of colouring among the foliage, bluish willows shading with gloomy beeches and golden walnuts, arrested and enchanted her eyes. Everywhere was an appearance of elegance and wealth—'elegance, the work of Nature, not of man, and opulence, the immediate gift of God and not the result of commerce.' Her appreciation of the Alps is noteworthy from its date: 'I look back on the majestic boundaries of Italy,' she wrote at Turin, 'with amazement at his courage who first profaned them. Surely the immediate sensation conveyed to the mind by the sight of such tremendous appearances must be in every traveller the same, a sensation of fulness never experienced before, a satisfaction that there is something great to be seen on earth, some object capable of contenting even fancy.' While bearing in mind that Rousseau had already written, one is struck by the modernity of the passage. It is true that the view is still *external;* it lacks the mysterious sense of interdependence between man and nature which makes Obermann belong so much to us and so little to his contemporaries. On the hills, says Obermann, where the heavens are immense, the air more still and life more permanent, nature eloquently expresses a vaster order, a more visible harmony: 'Là, l'hŏmme retrouve sa forme altérable mais indestructible; il respire l'air sauvage loin des émanations sociales; son être est à lui comme à l'univers: il vit d'une vie réelle dans l'unité sublime.' Here is a note undivined by Mrs. Piozzi, but she was keenly alive to the outward aspects of mountain landscape: the lovely auburn tints, the torrents bursting from the naked rocks, the little churches perched on steep ledges with their tinkling bells calling the quiet Savoyards to prayer. She declares that even the peasants who carried her *chaise-à-porteurs* seemed to take a new pleasure every time they beheld these glorious scenes, as they called one another's attention to the small changes that had taken place since last they passed. She came upon one peasant who spoke excellent English, having occupied a good position as gentleman's servant in England, but the longing for his native hills overpowered him, and he had thrown up all to return to them.

On the way the travellers stopped at Lyons, where they were excited by stories of animal magnetism, or hypnotism, as we should say, for the phenomena related are strictly of that order. Mrs. Piozzi hoped that 'a buffoonery so mean and a practice so diabolical' would not get into England. What would she have said to the new class of invalids, who, having allowed themselves to be hypnotized in haste, are occupied in repenting at leisure—to the two Russian girls of good family, who were lately placed in the care of Professor Branchi, of Naples, for treatment on account of hypnotic trances, which come on simultaneously in each, even when they are apart? Mrs. Piozzi's common-sense enabled her to see that the style of entertainment, then a novel one, was calculated to bring about scarcely amusing results.

She deserves praise for liking Turin—' this lovely little city,' she calls it—in contrast with the indifference or dislike of most travellers, from Montaigne downwards. Here she first saw an Italian opera acted in an Italian theatre, a box having been lent to her by Prince della Cisterna, one of whose descendants was to wear for a while the inauspicious crown of Spain. Here, on the threshold of Italy, every pleasure that politeness could invent or kindness bestow was held out for her acceptance; here Italian hospitality first consoled her for the fatigues of her journey, nor was the promise belied along all the road, for she received everywhere a full measure of the courtesy and attention lavished on British travellers in Italy until their quantity, and perhaps their quality, made it impossible to go on opening all doors as a matter of course to every wandering Englishman. Questions of rank and position were waived in their favour. Mrs. Piozzi confided to her friends on her return to England that in Lombardy people could never quite make out how she could be a lady when her first husband was a brewer—a dreadful piece of intelligence for those who affected to consider the immaculate Thrale connection damaged by the Piozzi alliance. The perplexity, however, did not interfere with the honour done to the witty and charming visitor, who manifests a gratitude which has not always been the kind of coin paid back by foreigners for Italian cordialities.

Gabriele Piozzi had been acquainted from his boyhood with the Marquis d'Aracieli, a nobleman of Spanish extraction, who lived in Milan. How the marquis came to know the Brescian lad is not explained, but he seems to have looked upon him in the light of a *protégé* from the time when Piozzi ran away from home because his family wanted to make him a priest. On that occasion he took refuge in the Palazzo Aracieli, and he again took refuge there when Mrs. Thrale had been worried into dismissing him, as it appeared, finally. He was the guest of the marquis when he was recalled, though sorely against the grain, by her relations, on their becoming convinced that she would succumb to the strain of the renunciation. It was natural that the Piozzis should choose Milan for their longest stay, as this acquaintance gave them at once the *entrée* to Milanese society. Mrs. Piozzi set to work to observe the features of the life around her, and noted things honestly as they looked to her, without malice, if at times not wholly without that shade of caricature which a clever writer, and especially a clever woman, finds it hard to resist. To say that her conclusions at times need correction, is only to say that she shared an infirmity common to the most intelligent painters of foreign manners. Take up a foreign book on English society, or a foreign newspaper which contains English gossip, and one is mostly struck by the topsy-turveydom of the writer's standpoint, even when his facts are right. Foreigners are apt to be led astray even more by what they hear than by what they see; they judge the general from the particular, accepting as final the first view or argument presented to them. Thus, when a young matron of the bourgeoise class announces that her *cavalier servente* pays her bills, Mrs. Piozzi jumps at the idea that this is a common practice, whereas she might have learnt from the old rhyme:

> 'Cavalier servente,
> Cavalier serpente,
> Cavalier del dente,'

that the 'knight of the tooth' was reputed to receive more favours than he conferred. He was frequently a humble relative—in every family were cadets too poor to marry (as they could not work for their living), too worldly or too sincere to become priests —to whom cavalier servitude secured a dinner, at any rate, if they wanted one. It was the custom to go to the theatre every evening—the box at the opera was an integral part of the household arrangements, a continuation of the salon—only it could not be reached by ladies without an escort. The chaperon did not exist, because a woman, however old, was no escort for another woman, nor could she herself dispense with an attendant of the other sex. A dowager of sixty and a bride of sixteen had equally to stay at home if there was not a man to accompany them. The cavalier's service was particularly in request at the theatre, but he was more or less on duty whenever his lady left her house for any purpose, with the doubtful exception of going to church. No husband outside a honeymoon could be expected to perform all these functions; he therefore appointed or agreed in the appointment of somebody else to act as his substitute.

This was in nine cases out of ten the eminently unromantic cavalier servitude of fact. The high-flown complimentary language, the profound bowing and hand-kissing of the period, combined to mystify strangers as to its real significance. Sometimes when there was really a lover in the question, the *cavalier servente* must have been a serious impediment; he was always 'là planté . . . à contrecarrer un pauvre tiers,' in the words of the witty Président de Brosses, who, though he did not wholly credit the assurances he received as to the invariable innocence of the institution, was yet far from passing on it the sweeping judgment arrived at by most foreigners. There is little doubt that habit and opportunity did, now and then, prove too strong for the two individuals thrown so constantly together. 'Juxtaposition is great,' as Clough says, in his 'Amours de Voyage'; but that such lapses represented the rule rather than the exception, is not borne out by either reason or record.

The institution had another variety, an ideal phase: as long as it was in vogue, it provided a frame for those deep and enduring friendships between men and women, which are of the pleasantest things offered by humanity to the gaze of angels. They did not begin nor did they end with it, but it formed their setting while it lasted. If anyone smiles at the word friendship, as applied to the relations of the sexes under a southern sun, he need only be reminded of Michael Angelo and Vittoria Colonna. A nation 'capable of impressions at once sudden and durable'—which is one of the best characterizations of the Italians ever made —is by its temperament not less, but more, than others fitted for affections, the permanency of which demands an unusual measure of intensity and patience. Later on in her travels, when staying in a palace near Bergamo, Mrs. Piozzi came upon the traces of one such friendship: 'The last nobleman who resided here,' she writes, 'father to the present lord, was *cavalier servente* to the immortal Clelia Borromeo, whose virtues and varieties of excellence would fill a volume.' The son still spoke of her death with tears in his eyes, and delighted in nothing more than in paying just tribute to her memory.

The Countess Clelia was one of a triad of illustrious women who honoured their sex in Italy in the first half of the eighteenth century. The other two were Laura Bassi, professor of philosophy at the University of Bologna, and Gaetana Agnesi, who at twenty discussed abstruse mathematical problems in Latin with many of the first scientific men of the time, and whom Mrs. Piozzi might have known at Milan, for she was still living there in 1784; but she had then for many years devoted all her energies to nursing and helping the poor and sick, which had been the dream of her brilliant and courted girlhood. The Président de Brosses' account of Gaetana Agnesi, whom he met in fear and trembling of a blue-stocking, but whom he found to be simple and winning as she was gifted, allows us to guess what Italian society lost by the almost total absence of young girls. Gaetana was a genius, and many who have won the name of saint have deserved it less; but the most commonplace young girl, if she be natural, high-spirited and easily amused, does more to raise the moral standard of society than the preaching of an army of divines. We laugh at the 'young person;' we ought to be grateful to her. In the Italy of that day, the young married woman who had just left her convent school, knowing no more of evil than a child of five, was suddenly separated by an impassable barrier from her girl companions, who would still have been her most congenial friends, and launched among married women of all ages, and married and unmarried men, whose conversation, if not their conduct, was not marked by reserve. Her own unmarried sister, even if by chance older than she was, would not have been allowed to go and stay in her house. All this is passing away, but there are relics of it left, since many kind and affectionate parents still think it their duty to send their daughters from seven to seventeen to some convent, which they never leave even for holidays. Another drawback to a healthy state of morality was the idleness of the married women; the servants being almost all men, household management fell to the master, not to the mistress, who was not occupied with the children, as they were sent out to nurse for the first two or three years of their lives, left to servants for the next three or four; and then, if they were girls, despatched to the inevitable convent till they married, or if boys, either sent to a school without holidays, or handed over to a clerical tutor till they went to the University.

While Mrs. Piozzi was inclined to criticise both theory and practice in the matter of conjugal relations, she noticed with surprise the extreme respect paid to family ties. Even distant kinsfolk commanded, in the younger generation, a care and deference hardly shown to parents in England. She attributes this to the less adventurous spirit of a people that had small interest in the government or larger affairs of the community, each individual being isolated in a little world, which to him was paramount. The spread of enterprise and a more liberal rule would, she thought, go to lessen or destroy the clannish sentiment then predominant and now, as a matter of fact, disappearing; but the reverential love of children for their parents, and especially of sons for their mothers, which so greatly charmed her, must still impress all who have access to the inner life of Italian families. She often returns to the subject ; when present at a Christmas party in Germany, where she saw the Christmas tree, and the other elaborate preparations for the amusement of the little ones, she says that she sat trying in vain to find out the reason why paternal affection seems so much warmer in Protestant countries, and filial piety in those which remain faithful to the Church of Rome. Would she think that the rapid progress of baby-worship in Italy has anything to do with the weakened authority of the successor of St. Peter?

Our author remarks on the rigid distinctions of rank, and at the same time the familiarity allowed between servants or dependents and their masters—two things that frequently co-existed. Tom Purdies are rare in a democracy. Not only dependents, but also the members of the little bourgeoisie who were brought in contact with great families, were treated, within stated limits, with the friendliness of genuine good feeling, and it was the habit of all to speak to those below themselves 'with a graciousness not often used by English men and women, even to their equals.' It is often said now in Italy that there is less real mixing of the classes than formerly, because when everyone considers himself on an equality with his host or passing acquaintance, people narrow their intercourse to the number of persons they are willing to accept on these terms, and strictly keep the rest at a distance.

'High people,' says Mrs. Piozzi, 'took an infinite pleasure in seeing the masses amuse themselves; in England it was thought vulgar to be merry when the mob was so.' It might be suggested that the mob in Italy makes merry in a fashion less harassing to the artistic sense than did its counterpart in England in the last century. The crowd even on an Italian racecourse exhibits no rowdy or boisterous elements. On the other hand, a fine mind will enjoy the harmless enjoyment of others, whatever be its form; Margate on a summer day presents a spectacle which ought to be as gratifying to the inward vision as any Italian *festa*, though it be less picturesque. Besides, Margate (taking Margate as a type) is not vulgar; since the essence of vulgarity is the desire to seem what you are not, and nowhere is this desire less to the fore than on those yellow sands. Mrs. Piozzi speaks more than once of the notable absence of this essential vulgarity among the Italians of her day: the poor did not try to appear rich, nor did the rich ape the airs of nobility if they had it not; money was not worshipped, nor was the want of it ridiculed; in conversation there was no straining after effect, or pretence to a scholarship or cleverness not really possessed. Politeness sprang from the wish to be helpful or to give pleasure, not from the wish to shine.

Mrs. Piozzi admired the excellent arrangements for the comfort of the audience in Italian theatres, where each box was like a private boudoir, but she did not care for the performances, and complained of the same piece being given night after night. The ballet—no mere display of dancing, but a story told in pantomime—was then, as it has remained, an important feature; and few who have seen these ballets, admirably acted and put on the stage as they are at the Scala or San Carlo, can wonder at the praise bestowed on them by Shelley and other Englishmen. Mrs. Piozzi, however, was not amused by this sort of entertainment, and her distaste for it reached its climax when she saw the ballet of Don Giovanni, 'a horrible history,' which she suspected might be partly true (as, indeed, it was), and which she thought anyhow too shocking for the stage. Did she relent when Mozart, a few years later, gave the legend a new and splendid lease of theatrical existence?

The Piozzis went into Venetia by Cremona and Mantua: they do not seem to have ever gone to Brescia, Piozzi's home, though it lay hardly at all out of their route. Nevertheless, it is pretty certain that Piozzi, who was much attached to his father, saw him while in Italy; probably he invited him to Milan. He may have shrunk from imposing on his family, who were not rich, the expense of receiving the *signora inglese*, words which to an Italian ear suggest somebody who cannot do without comforts and luxuries which even the wealthy in Italy often dispense with.

At Venice the sweetness of manners, dialect and address won Mrs. Piozzi's heart at once. She had doubted the truth of the assertion that the gondoliers sang stanzas from Tasso and Ariosto, but her incredulity was dispelled at the very moment that she committed it to writing, for the gondolier under her window began singing 'to an odd sort of tune,' the flight of Erminia in the 'Gerusalemme.' So they sang on, till the independence of Venice was bartered away at Campo Formio, when they hushed their songs, and in the long term of servitude, Tasso was well-nigh forgotten, but Ariosto, if not sung, is still read aloud in the evenings at Chioggia to an admiring crowd of fisher folk.

The contrasts between splendour and squalid want had given Mrs. Piozzi a bad impression of the republican institutions at Genoa, but the venerable Republic of Venice found in her a warm admirer.

Her remarks are not without interest, because it is the historical fashion to regard Venice before its fall as in the last stage of decadent senility. Mrs. Piozzi was no politician, but she had her eyes open, and what she saw was not degeneracy. The senators, if they amused themselves all night, were at their posts to the minute in the morning, and their attention to the affairs of State was unremitting; gaiety and love of pleasure were combined with the most serious concern for the commonweal, which was shared by all classes from the highest to the lowest. The Venetians were less prejudiced and more tolerant than other Italians, which the English observer has the penetration to explain by the fact that they were happier. Patriotism, she declares, was inherent in the breast of every citizen: '"Dulce et decorum est pro patria mori," seems a sentence grown obsolete in other Italian States, but it is still in full force here; and I doubt not but the high-born and high-souled ladies of this day would willingly, as did their generous ancestors in 1600, part with their rings, bracelets, every ornament, to make ropes for those ships which defend their dearer country.' Mrs. Piozzi was not mistaken; in 1849 the Venetian ladies did sacrifice their jewels and all their treasures to prolong the defence of Venetian liberty.

That passage, which has almost the dignity of a prophecy, may be taken as making part amends for the writer's more than indifference to the servile condition of Lombardy and Tuscany. ''Tis dull,' she says, 'to hear people lament the want of liberty.' The pleasure of an English sojourner at Florence was diminished by the incessant complaints of a government he did not understand and of oppression he could not remedy. Was it the measures or the men, she wondered, that lay at the root of the discontent? Were they to have one of the old Medici back, would not the Florentines go to bed quietly enough when he told them? If these were her reflections in Tuscany, at Milan Mrs. Piozzi was still more impatient of criticism passed on the double-headed eagle, over which bird she became almost sentimental. It has, in justice, to be allowed that the rule of the House of Hapsburg in Italy in the eighteenth century was not what it was in the nineteenth. If there was petty interference in Tuscany, and in Lombardy the arrogance of a power which thought itself invulnerable, of despotism in the worst sense there was little or none. Austria in Italy in the eighteenth century reformed many glaring abuses, and at that time was on the eve of abolishing the Inquisition both in the north and centre. Yet she was still an alien mistress, and a feeling was growing, steadily if slowly, that of such Italy had seen enough. One would like to find the sympathies of the English visitor enlisted on the side of these nascent hopes, but to expect to find them there would be to misconceive the temper of contemporary English opinion. An enormous change had to come about before an Englishman could write lines that were penned while Mrs. Piozzi was still alive, but which belong to another epoch: 'I shall think it by far the most interesting spectacle and moment in existence, to see the Italians send the barbarians of all nations back to their dens. It is no great matter, supposing Italy could be liberated, who or what is sacrificed. It is a grand object—the very poetry of politics. Only think, a free Italy! Why, there has been nothing like it since the days of Augustus.' He who wrote thus was the first to leave off talking of 'irrevocable dooms' and 'final days'; and he was prepared to give his money and his life as a warrant of his sincerity. Byron may have been as bad a poet as those who ought to know now assure us that he was, but he may count on the lasting gratitude of two nations, if his own forget him.

Mrs. Piozzi was sensible of the perennial charm which for Shakespeare's countrymen the cities of Venetia, and Venice most of all, must always derive

Introduction

from his genius. 'To an English traveller,' she says, 'each place presents ideas originally suggested by Shakespeare, of whom nature and truth are the perpetual mirrors. Other authors remind one of things which one has seen in life, but the scenes of life themselves remind one of Shakespeare. When I first looked on the Rialto, with what immediate images did it not supply me?' Not even the hackneyed ritornello of a century of ciceroni and guide-books has succeeded in spoiling the magic; the air of these cities remains redolent of the poet's creations. What if Juliet's tomb be a washtub? Does not every cypress at Verona mourn for her? Are not the pomegranates full of nightingales, and the misty mountain-tops—do they not await the day? About nightingales, by-the-bye, Mrs. Piozzi says that they sing less well than in England, and only in the early morning; but in spots where they thrive they sing both night and day, and far later into the summer than their English relations, who probably get hoarse sooner owing to the climate. As to excellence, there is a vast difference between individuals, and the finest singer cannot display his skill to advantage save in perfect silence; but, granted the right bird in the right place, and Virgil's nightingales need fear no rivals.

. Mrs. Piozzi writes intelligently on the dialects of

the different States, and, while rightly assigning the palm to pure Tuscan (especially as spoken at Siena, where she was in raptures with the grace and propriety of expression even of the humblest folk), she does not fail to seize the force, raciness, and exactitude of shading found in the *patois* used by the other populations. She traces the diversity of speech to the political divisions of the country; but dialect dies hard, notwithstanding political unity, compulsory education and military service. There is at present a greatly increased knowledge of Italian; yet the provincials, whatever be their class, still speak their own familiar idiom when alone. Each separate dialect is a bond of union, a free-masonry, an echo from home in distant parts—home, which in Italy is less an emotion of the hearth than of the sunlight as it falls upon the native valley, the village campanile, the piazza with the plane-trees and the bowling-ground, the fountain with the brown-armed girls. Not only does there exist the broad distinctions from the Doric of Naples to the sweet lisp of Venice, but within the space of a few square miles three or four hamlets may each have a peculiar lingo of which the differences, though not to be distinguished by strangers, are sufficient to indicate the birthplace of anyone speaking it to a practised ear. He must be an inveterate devotee of uniformity who would wish altogether away these articulate landmarks, these reflections of the life-history of each little community. As long as people speak dialect, they speak a language which they have invented and which they understand; whilst when they speak the last literary or journalistic casting of the standard tongue, the poor, and not the poor only, are commonly trying to frame their ideas in terms that convey as little natural sense to their minds as if they were endeavouring to speak Chinese.

It must strike the reader that in her few references to rustic life, Mrs. Piozzi gives an impression of prosperity and cheerfulness of which the first, if not the second, has sadly declined. She admires the always beautiful and often rich peasant costumes that are to be seen now only in those few districts where their use has been capriciously retained. There is hardly a trace of costume in Sicily, but the Calabrian goatherds still wear their smart velvet doublets and pendent caps; in the North, the blue petticoats bordered with red of the Amazonian women of the Val Mastalone, and the 'silver' worn in the hair of the marriageable girls in the Novarese plains, remain to tell of days when in each place there was a traditional mode of dress with appropriate ornaments, which were handed down as heirlooms from mother to daughter.

There is a rhyming Italian proverb which, though Mrs. Piozzi does not quote it, she certainly acted upon: 'Chi vuol vivere e star bene, prenda il mondo come viene.' She took the world as it came, made slight of small inconveniences, liked Italian cookery (the soup, she says, in the poorest hut was better than what was often placed on the tables of the rich in England), and did not even grumble much at the cold comfort of Italian houses in winter, which may have contributed towards making the 'plant man' more vigorous in Italy than elsewhere, but which was then a sad trial to visitors from Northern lands, and is so now to those who become intimate with good old-fashioned Italian families that preserve the ancient horror of stoves and fires, and concede at most the use of the *scaldino*, the little warming-pan full of hot embers to be placed under the feet. Content was our traveller's principle and practice. She remarks: 'How little do those ladies consult their own interest who make impatience of petty inconveniences their best supplement for conversation, fancy themselves more important as less contented, and imagine all delicacy to consist in the difficulty of being pleased.' Only two things really put her out—the scorpions and the mosquitoes. The misery of Florence was, she said, that the climate was so good that all animals flourished in it—gnats in particular. At the Bagni di Pisa scorpions were the order of the day ; a ragged boy obligingly cleared the kitchen of seventeen while the English lady's maid stood in contemplation on a chair. For once Mrs. Piozzi was 'fairly driven wild.' Seventeen scorpions are a good many, but her extreme fear of their sting seems exaggerated, as, except in the far south, not much comes of it, unless the blood is already in a bad state. Other creatures there were that were more to her taste—the fireflies, for instance, and the engaging little lizards about which she was quite ready to believe the pretty story of their warning men of the approach of venomous snakes. That this was true, Mrs. Piozzi was assured by some of those eye-witnesses which the miraculous never lacks.

A bright picture is given of Count Mannucci's country-seat near Prato : the society so cheerful, the climate so splendid, the prospects over the glorious country so wonderful. Mrs. Piozzi did not see much of Italian country-life, but what she did see charmed her as it had charmed Lady Mary Wortley Montagu by its gaiety, good-humour and unconventional ease. It is to be regretted that south of Florence she carried no introductions, and did not stay long enough in any place to make acquaintances, so that we lose the glimpses of Italian interiors which add to the value of her earlier and also of her later reminiscences. In Rome, besides lacking the opportunity of observing native life, she was at first rather overawed by the greatness of her surroundings. 'In this town' (she writes), 'unlike to every other, the things take my attention all away from the people; while in every other the people had much more of my mind employed on them than the things.' So she became more learned and less amusing. At Naples she recovers her vivacity, and it was just like her to stumble upon her old French hairdresser turned hermit half-way up Vesuvius. She mentions that when the mountain was *cattiva*, it was thought to depend on the number of heretics who had lately ascended it. So Lalande asserted that on one occasion when the liquefaction of St. Januarius' blood proceeded slowly, the authorities had the idea that the presence of a heretic, the English consul, might be the cause. With the greatest civility, they invited him to permit them to show him some object of interest outside the church, and no sooner was he clear of the building than the miracle accomplished itself to the general relief.

Mrs. Piozzi was shocked by the habit of the lower orders of tattooing their bodies all over with strange devices, a custom still carried to extraordinary lengths in Southern Italy, most of all among the

doubtful classes, as came to light in the recent
'Mala Vita' trials at Bari. She observed, with
more good-nature than he merited, the lazarone
king, who from the boor he was then, pandering
to the lower tastes of his lower subjects, not even
from policy but from choice, was to become in a few
years the brutal and faithless monarch England
knew too well. She thinks him popular, as no doubt
he was, among the class he imitated, but she notes
how the mob had no scruple in throwing large
stones after him every time he ran away from an
eruption. She notes, too, that his Majesty 'most
wisely' kept eight thousand soldiers in St. Elmo,
ready to bombard the town at the shortest notice,
confiding the command to Austrian or Spanish
officers, who would have no tenderness in handling
the Neapolitan population in a revolt. She remarks
that the Neapolitan masses, though superstitious,
are not afraid of the supernatural, that they do not
care about ghosts, and sleep composedly in the
catacombs where a stout-hearted Englishman might
be excused for having bad dreams. Their sun is too
bright, their twilight too brief, and they are themselves too truly of the ancient world for their own
shadows to terrify them. Then, too, the Neapolitan
is a fatalist, and if fatalism be not the source of the
highest courage, it produces a good sort of workaday

stolidity adapted to people who live in the presence of perils over which they can have no command.

Connected with this fatalism is the happy-go-lucky spirit in which the Neapolitan builds again and again on the slopes of Vesuvius swept by the lava streams. If things go wrong he beats his saints, or, perhaps, reproaches himself with not having done adequate honour to them. Yet he has qualities as well as defects; who so kindly as he, when his blood is not up; who so frugal and patient? There have been signs at Naples of the resolute public opinion which is of all things the most wanted in Italy: the proposal to establish the Inquisition was extinguished by one breath of popular disfavour, and not many years ago, to give a trifling but significant instance, a miserable woman known only from having figured in a murder trial, was summarily hissed off the Neapolitan stage after receiving applause in Rome. The worst points of these children of the sun come largely from the superior cleverness left to them by their Greek ancestors, which, finding no other field for activity, has reduced crime to a fine art. Pity that though lazaroni kings who run away from eruptions are gone for ever, a way has yet to be discovered of clearing Southern Italy of the moral weeds which prevent the good seed from bringing forth its fruit.

During Mrs. Piozzi's visit there was a performance at one of the Neapolitan theatres of 'Il Re Lear e le sue tre figlie,' and elsewhere she heard of plays with Shakespearean subjects. Though Shakespeare no longer means bankruptcy in England, it is doubtful if he is so often on the boards in one form or another at home as in Italy. Ernesto Rossi's repertory ranges from 'Hamlet' to 'Julius Cæsar'; Salvini still thrills the Florentines on great occasions with his wonderful Othello. Eleonora Duse has made a brilliant study of Cleopatra, and in poor little out-of-the-way villages you see every day posted up scrawled handbills with some such announcement as this, taken from Coccaglio: 'Romeo o le tombe di Verona.' Mrs. Piozzi missed the 'Lear,' but she witnessed an exclusively Neapolitan spectacle—the 'Triumph of Policinello,' as, surmounting a pyramid of twenty-eight men, that personage was drawn through the town on a car to which were harnessed eight beautiful white oxen. She feels sure that his name is derived from flea (pulce), for, she says, the mask in which he appears 'is cut and coloured so exactly to resemble a flea, with hook nose and wrinkles.' The etymology is original, and may be as good as any other, although the name is generally referred to Puccio d'Aniello, an actor who once represented the part. The Italians abound in nicknames, and the nickname soon becomes better known than the actual surname, which an Italian peasant can never remember; but the origin of these innumerable pseudonyms is quickly lost beyond recall.

The graceful and high-spirited horses attracted Mrs. Piozzi's attention, as did the skill and pride in horsemanship, for which the Neapolitans had been known from the time when Portia's suitor from Naples talked of nothing but his horse. Our author was desperately tempted to buy—not a horse —but a donkey. She never longed for anything so much in her life, but dared not carry out her wish lest she should be laughed at. Visitors to the South will sympathize with her: who has not fallen in love with the enchanting little donkeys of Sicily, no bigger than St. Bernard dogs? Mrs. Piozzi's knack of picking up information is illustrated by her noting that canine madness is almost unknown at Naples, an exemption she thinks due to the abundance of water, but water can hardly be said to have been abundant there until the present excellent supply was introduced after the cholera epidemic of 1884. Most authorities believe that in the multitude of Southern dogs lies their safety, the conditions of their life being more natural. At all events their immunity continues, while rabies rages in the north of the country.

The carnival was going on when Mrs. Piozzi returned to Rome, and on this second visit she looked about her more to the reader's advantage than when employed in sight-seeing. She was pleasantly impressed by the Pope (Angelo Braschi, known as Pius VI.), whose air of sweetness and majesty well suited his position. She wished him long life and prosperity, but cites, in joke, a Latin prediction then current in Rome—suggested, perhaps, by zephyr blowing on a flower, which figured in the Pope's arms—to the effect that 'the days are coming when Braschi will have nothing left to him but the wind'; which is just what happened, for Pius VI. died an exile's death at Valence. The Romans have not lost their Sibylline habit: some of their doggerel oracles in this century have turned out curiously correct, as the 'Massimiliano non ti fidare,' which was on the lips of all the Roman people when that ill-fated prince went to Mexico.

In a few years, Mrs. Piozzi expected that no one would be called upon to kiss the Pope's toe—a ceremony she deemed inconsistent with his character as a Christian priest. The form is still gone through by the faithful; and Pio Nono, when he saw Protestants standing stiffly at his receptions, used to ask who were those statues?—a well-merited rebuke, as it would be difficult to know what they went to do in that *galère*. With regard to the eagerness of the Roman poor to receive the papal benediction, Mrs. Piozzi recalls the case of an old Welsh farmer, who went a long way to obtain the bishop's blessing, because he thought it would be good for his rheumatism. So in Ireland, the clergy of the Disestablished Church are to this day credited with some of the marvellous powers liberally attributed to their Catholic brethren—only the Nonconformist minister can work no magic. The Irish peasant seems vaguely to accept the validity of the English orders, while thinking that Anglican doctrine leads to perdition. Who can tell all the various reckonings based upon a blessing? A few years since, a priest from the country, at one of Leo XIII.'s receptions, proffered for benediction a small closed box. 'Che cosa contiene?' asked the Pope, to whom the answer appeared evasive as he passed the box over. What was in it? Possibly something very innocent, but one cannot help recollecting the crucifix of Crema with its hidden stiletto. Mrs. Piozzi, for her part, was content with the humble benediction of an old Armenian father, whose black robe and white beard had fascinated her as he said mass every day before one particular altar at St. Peter's. He observed her interest in his appearance, and afterwards, when they met by chance in the street, he always stood still to bless her. This must have been one of the earliest of the Armenian monks to take up his residence in Italy, where they remain to this day respected and liked by all.

She says that the Italians are glad to have got rid of the Jesuits, who were expelled in 1769—why, she does not know. She would herself be disposed to regret their departure. 'Nothing can be wilder,' in her opinion, than the usual conventual education for children not intended for the cloister, but the Jesuits, being men of the world and acquainted with its requirements, would appear well qualified for the office of teacher. The same defence has often been taken up since, and would be unanswerable were it not that human perversity mistrusts the worldly wisdom of the great society.

Mrs. Piozzi left Rome and began her homeward journey on April 19th, 1786. The tulips carpeted the Campagna, and she compared them with the British harebell. Here, she says, we have Italy and England summed up. She rather spoils the comparison by adding that, with cultivation, the harebell becomes a hyacinth, which shows that she makes the common confusion between the pretty *Scilla nutans* of the woods and the real campanula. The words that follow—about the fragrant hedges of Kent and Surrey, the primroses and budding horse-chestnuts—are evidence that the writer had a fit of the spring nostalgia, of which most English wanderers know the attack :

> 'Oh, to be in England
> Now that April's there !'

Who has not had the feeling, though were he in England he would be bewailing the east winds ? The mind is more sensitive to pain than to pleasure at the moment, to pleasure than to pain in the retrospect, which is why almost everyone imagines that his childhood and his childhood's home were happy.

The Piozzis journeyed north by the Adriatic coast, and several pages are given to a description of Loreto, with its still unrifled treasury. Mrs. Piozzi reports a conversation with a learned ecclesiastic, who said that they none of them believed that the Santa Casa was what it is represented to be, but that since it had been for so long the object of veneration of the wisest and best Christians, and even of the Turks, he thought that it was well to abstain from mockery. It is questionable if learned ecclesiastics would now venture on so frank a statement. If Mrs. Piozzi did not adopt the theory of edification versus truth, her last look at the famous shrine brings to mind one of those scenes the infinite charm of which gets round the sceptical conscience, be it never so robust. She saw troops of pilgrims winding slowly up the hillside from the lovely sea, singing as they went most sweetly, with now and then a woman's voice soaring above the rest. Were the beautiful indeed the splendour of the true, what better argument could be desired than the beauty of such scenes?

Journeying north, the Piozzis stayed again at most of the former places, as well as at some new ones, and we meet with the entertaining little sketches of intimate life which enlivened the early part of the tour. Mrs. Piozzi lent her English maid to a lady who wished to be initiated into the secrets of clear-starching, but who, when she saw all the pains and nicety required, burst out laughing at so unnecessary an expenditure of trouble, while her servants crossed themselves in all the corners of the room. Anyone who has kept house in Italy will smile, or possibly weep, over this anecdote. But it would be a mistake to conclude that Italians are incapable of delicate or persevering work; Italian agriculture needs an amount of patient skill undreamt of by the English labourer; the cultivation of vines, olives, silkworms, and lemons is in each case a separate and arduous study. Again, as everyone knows, in painting walls and ceilings, the commonest Italian workman shows a *disinvoltura* that would astonish the British artisan.

On the other hand, ask your gardener to keep your flower-beds in the order in which they would be kept even in an English cottage-garden, and he esteems you an irrational person. Most likely, after all, it is a matter of inherited habits. The hedge-sparrow makes his nest in one way and the long-tailed tit in another. Mrs. Piozzi saw a great tall fellow ironing his mistress's best *fichu* with a warming-pan, but she admits that the lady looked as lovely when her toilette was performed as if its preparation had been less barbarous. The grace of Italian women is independent of accessories; a few natural flowers, arranged with the taste that never deserts them when they trust to themselves and do not imitate, become them better than jewels.

At Lugano Mrs. Piozzi writes cheerfully: 'Here was the first gallows I have seen these two years.' She often complains of the mildness of the law in Italy, and of that compassion for criminals which Professor Lombroso has twisted into a science by proclaiming them irresponsible. There are more serious grounds now than in the last century for doubting whether mercy is not carried to an excess in dealing with Italian delinquents, for the administration of justice was then in most countries so ruthless that what seemed leniency would seem severity to us.

It is not needful to follow Mrs. Piozzi across Germany and Belgium, to Calais and Dover, but it should be recorded that she kept her good-humour to the end; happy to set out, she was happier to return, and she came back from this prolonged wedding-tour as satisfied with the companion of her travels and of her life as when she started. It would be cynical to add 'which happens rarely,' but honesty compels the addition 'which does not always happen.' The reader is likely to catch something of her good spirits; if he does so, he may rest assured that he could not have spent an idle hour more wisely than in turning over the leaves of these extracts from the long-forgotten volumes of 'Observations in a Journey through Italy.'

CHAPTER I

TURIN AND GENOA

The Alps—Turin—Dr. Allioni and the Fossil Trout—Family Fondness—Italian Cookery—Crowded Habitations—Genoa—Devotion and Morals—Beggars—A Rural Theatre—Poor Nobles.

October 17th, 1784.

WE have at length passed the Alps, and are safely arrived at this lovely little city, whence I look back on the majestic boundaries of Italy, with amazement at his courage who first profaned them. Surely the immediate sensation conveyed to the mind by the sight of such tremendous appearances must be in every traveller the same, a sensation of fulness never experienced before, a satisfaction that there is something great to be seen on earth—some object capable of contenting even fancy.

I had the satisfaction of seeing a chamois at a distance, and spoke with a fellow who had killed five hungry bears that made depredation on his pastures: we looked on him with reverence as a monster-tamer of antiquity, Hercules or Cadmus; he had the skin of a beast wrapped round his middle, which confirmed the fancy; but our servants, who borrowed from no fictitious records the few ideas that adorned their talk, told us he reminded them of John the Baptist. I had scarce recovered the shock of this too sublime comparison, when we approached his cottage, and found the felons nailed against the wall, like foxes' heads or spread kites in England. Here are many goats, but neither white nor large like those which browse upon the steeps of Snowdon, or clamber among the cliffs of Plinlimmon.

I chatted with a peasant in the Haute Morienne concerning the endemial swelling of the throat which is found in seven out of every ten persons here; he told me what I had always heard, but do not yet believe, that it was produced by drinking the snow-water. Certain it is these places are not wholesome to live in; most of the inhabitants are troubled with weak and sore eyes, and I recollect Sir Richard Jebb telling me, more than seven years ago, that when he passed through Savoy, the various applications made to him, either for the cure or prevention of blindness by numberless unfortunate wretches that crowded round him, hastened his quitting a province where such horrible complaints prevailed. One has heard it related that the goître or gozzo of the throat is reckoned a beauty by those who possess it; but I spoke with many, and all agreed to lament it as a misfortune. That it does really proceed merely from living in a snowy country would be well confirmed by accounts of a similar sickness being endemial in Canada; but of an American goître I have never yet heard — and Wales, methinks, is snowy enough and mountainous enough, God knows; yet were such an excrescence to be seen there, the people would never have done wondering and blessing themselves.

As for Mount Cenis, I never felt myself more hungry or better enjoyed a good dinner than I did upon its top: but the trout in the lake there have been over-praised; their pale colour allured me but little in the first place, nor is their flavour equal to that of trout found in running water. Going down the Italian side of the Alps is, after all, an astonishing journey, and affords the most magnificent scenery in nature, which, varying at every step, gives new impression to the mind each moment of one's passage; while the portion of terror excited either by real or fancied dangers on the way, is just sufficient to mingle with the pleasure and make one feel the full effect of sublimity. To the chairmen who carry one, though nothing can be new, it is observable that the glories of these objects have never faded.

I heard them speak to each other of their beauties, and the change of light since they had passed by last time, while a fellow who spoke English as well as a native told us that, having lived in a gentleman's service twenty years between London and Dublin, he at length begged his discharge, choosing to retire and finish his days a peasant upon these mountains, where he first opened his eyes upon scenes that made all other views of nature insipid to his taste.

If impressions of beauty remain, however, those of danger die away by frequent reiteration; the men who carried me seemed amazed that I should feel any emotions of fear. 'Qu'est-ce donc, madame?'* was the coldly-asked question to my repeated injunction of 'Prenez garde!'†—not very apparently unnecessary neither, where the least slip must have been fatal both to them and me.

The avenue to Turin, most magnificently planted, and drawn in a wide, straight line, shaded like the Birdcage Walk in St. James's Park for twelve miles in length, is a dull work, but very useful and convenient in so hot a country. It has been completed by the taste and at the sole expense of his Sardinian majesty, that he may enjoy a cool shady drive from one of his palaces to the other. The town to which

* What's the matter, my lady?   † Take care.
(The translations throughout are Mr. Piozzi's.)

this long approach conveys one, does not disgrace its entrance. It is built in form of a star, with a large stone in its centre, on which you are desired to stand and see the streets all branch regularly from it, each street terminating with a beautiful view of the surrounding country, like spots of ground seen in many of the old-fashioned parks in England when the étoile and vista were the mode. I think there is still one subsisting even now, if I remember right, in Kensington Gardens.

This charming town is the salon of Italy; but it is a finely-proportioned and well-ornamented salon, happily constructed to call in the fresh air at the end of every street, through which a rapid stream is directed that ought to carry off all nuisances, which here have no apology for want of any convenience purchasable by money, and which must for that reason be the choice of inhabitants who would perhaps be too happy had they a natural taste for that neatness which might here be enjoyed in its purity. The arches formed to defend passengers from the rain and sun, which here might have even serious effects from their violence, deserve much praise; while their architecture, uniting our ideas of comfort and beauty together, form a traveller's taste, and teach him to admire that perfection of which a miniature may certainly be found at Turin, when once a police shall be established there to prevent such places being used for the very grossest purposes and polluted with smells that poison all one's pleasure.

Some letters from home directed me to inquire in this town for Dr. Charles Allioni, who kindly received and permitted me to examine the rarities of which he has a very capital collection. His fossil-fish in slate—blue slate—are surprisingly well preserved; but there is in the world, it seems, a crystallized trout, not flat nor the flesh eaten away, as I understand, but round, and, as it were, cased in crystal like our aspiques, or fruit in jelly, the colour still so perfect that you may plainly perceive the spots upon it, he says. To my inquiries after this wonderful petrefaction, he replied 'that it might be bought for a thousand pounds,' and added 'that if he were a ricco Inglese,* he would not hesitate for the price.'

'Where may I see it, sir?' said I; but to that question no entreaties could produce an answer after he once found I had no mind to buy.

That fresh-water fish have been known to remain locked in the flinty bosom of Monte Uda in Carnia, the academical discourse of Cyrillo di Cremona,

* Rich Englishman.

pronounced there in the year 1749, might have informed us; and we are all familiar, I suppose, with the anchor named in the fifteenth book of Ovid's 'Metamorphoses.' Strabo mentions pieces of a galley found three thousand stadii from any sea, and Dr. Allioni tells me that Monte Bolca has been long acknowledged to contain the fossils, now diligently digging out under the patronage of some learned naturalists at Verona. The trout, however, is of value much beyond these productions certainly, as it is closed round as if in a transparent case, we find, hermetically sealed by the soft hand of Nature, who spoiled none of her own ornaments in preserving them for the inspection of her favourite students.

The amiable old professor from whom these particulars were obtained, and who endured my teasing him in bad Italian for intelligence he cared not to communicate with infinite sweetness and patience, grew kinder to me as I became more troublesome to him; and, showing me the book upon botany to which he had just then put the last line, turned his dim eyes from me, and said, as they filled with tears:

'You, madam, are the last visitor I shall ever more admit to talk upon earthly subjects. My work is done; I finished it as you were entering. My business now is but to wait the will of God and die. Do you, who I hope will live long and happily, seek out your own salvation and pray for mine.'

Poor dear Dr. Allioni! My inquiries concerning this truly venerable mortal ended in being told that his relations and heirs teased him cruelly to sell his manuscripts, insects, etc., and divide the money amongst them before he died. An English scholar of the same abilities would be apt enough to despise such admonitions, and dispose at his own liking and leisure of what his industry alone had gained, his learning only collected; but there seems to be much more family fondness on the Continent than in our island—more attention to parents, more care for uncles and nephews, and sisters and aunts, than in a commercial country like ours, where for the most part each one makes his own way separate, and, having received little assistance at the beginning of life, considers himself as little indebted at the close of it.

Whoever takes a long journey, however he may at his first commencement be tempted to accumulate schemes of convenience and combinations of travelling niceties, will cast them off in the course of his travels as incumbrances; and whoever sets out in life, I believe, with a crowd of relations round him, will, on the same principle, feel disposed to drop one or two of them at every turn, as they hang about and impede his progress, and make his own game single-handed. I speak of Englishmen, whose religion and government inspire rather a spirit of public benevolence than contract the social affections to a point, and co-operate, besides, to prompt that genius for adventure and taste of general knowledge which has small chance to spring up in the inhabitants of a feudal State, where each considers his family as himself, and, having derived all the comfort he has ever enjoyed from his relations, resolves to return their favours at the end of a life which they make happy in proportion as it is so; and this accounts for the equality required in continental marriages, which are avowedly made here without regard to inclination, as the keeping up a family, not the choice of a companion, is considered as important; while the lady, bred up in the same notions, complies with her first duties, and considers the second as infinitely more dispensable.

Genoa, Nov. 1, 1784.

The sure-footed and docile mule, with which in England I was but little acquainted, here claims no small attention from his superior size and beauty. The disagreeable noise they make so frequently, however, hinders one from wishing to ride them; it is not braying somehow, but worse—it is neighing out of tune.

I have put nothing down about eating since we arrived in Italy, where no wretched hut have I yet entered that does not afford soup better than one often tastes in England even at magnificent tables. Game of all sorts—woodcocks in particular. Porporati, the so justly famed engraver, produced upon his hospitable board, one of the pleasant days we passed with him, a couple so exceedingly large, that I hesitated and looked again to see whether they were really woodcocks, till the long bill convinced me.

One reads of the luxurious emperors that made fine dishes of the little birds' brains, phenicopters' tongues, etc., and of the actor who regaled his guests with nightingale-pie, with just detestation of such curiosity and expense; but thrushes, larks, and blackbirds are so very frequent between Turin and Novi, I think they might serve to feed all the fantastical appetites to which Vitellius himself could give encouragement and example.

The Italians retain their tastes for small birds in full force, and consider beccafichi, ortolani, etc., as the most agreeable dainties. It must be confessed that they dress them incomparably. The sheep here are all lean and dirty-looking—few in number, too; but the better the soil the worse the mutton, we know, and here is no land to throw away, where every inch turns to profit in the olive-yards, vines, or something of much higher value than letting out to feed sheep.

Population seems much as in France, I think; but the families are not in either nation disposed according to British notions of propriety; all stuffed together into little towns and large houses (*entassées*, as the French call it), one upon another, in such a strange way, that were it not for the quantity of grapes on which the poor people live, with other acescent food enjoined by the Church, and doubtless suggested by the climate, I think putrid fevers must necessarily carry off crowds of them at once.

The head-dress of the women in this drive through some of the northern states of Italy varied at every post—from the velvet cap, commonly a crimson one, worn by the girls in Savoia, to the Piedmontese plait round the bodkin at Turin, and the odd kind of white wrapper used in the exterior provinces of the Genoese dominions. Uniformity of almost any sort gives a certain pleasure to the eye, and it seems an invariable rule in these countries that all the women of every district should dress just alike. It is the best way of making the men's task easy in judging which is handsomest; for taste so varies the human figure in France and England, that it is impossible to have an idea how many pretty faces and agreeable forms would lose and how many gain admirers in those nations, were a sudden edict to be published that all should dress exactly alike for a year. Meantime, since we left Dessein's, no such delightful place by way of inn have we yet seen as here at Novi. My chief amusement at Alexandria was to look out upon the *huddled* market-place, as a great dramatic writer of our day has called it; and who could help longing there for Zoffani's pencil to paint the lively scene?

Passing the Po by moonlight near Casale exhibited an entertainment of a very different nature, not unmixed with ill-concealed fear indeed, though the contrivance of crossing it is not worse managed than a ferry at Kew or Richmond used to be before our bridges were built. Bridges over the rapid Po would, however, be truly ridiculous; when swelled by the mountain snows, it tears down all before it in its fury and inundates the country round.

Genoa la Superba stands proudly on the margin of a gulf crowded with ships and resounding with voices which never fail to animate a British hearer —the sailor's shout, the mariner's call, swelled by successful commerce or strengthened by newly-acquired fame.

The Dorian palace is exceedingly fine; the Durazzo palace, for aught I know, is finer; and marble here seems like what one reads of silver in King Solomon's time, which, says the Scripture, 'was nothing counted of in the days of Solomon.' Casa Brignoli, too, is splendid and commodious; the terraces and gardens on the house-tops, and the fresco paintings outside, give one new ideas of human life, and exhibits a degree of luxury unthought on in colder climates. But here we live on green peas and figs the first day of November, while orange and lemon trees flaunt over the walls more common than pears in England.

The Balbi mansion, filled with pictures, detained us from the churches filled with more. I have heard some of the Italians confess that Genoa even pretends to vie with Rome herself in ecclesiastical splendour. In devotion, I should think, she would be with difficulty outdone; the people drop down on their knees in the street, and crowd to the church-doors while the benediction is pronouncing, with a zeal which one might hope would draw down stores of grace upon their heads. Yet I hear from the inhabitants of other provinces that they have a bad character among their neighbours, who love not the 'base Ligurian,' and accuse them of many immoralities. They tell one, too, of a disreputable saying here, how there are at Genoa men without honesty, women without modesty, a sea with no fish, and a wood with no birds. Birds, however, here certainly are by the million, and we have eaten fish since we came every day; but I am informed they are neither cheap nor plentiful, nor considered as excellent in their kinds. Here is macaroni enough, however! The people bring in such a vast dish of it at a time, it disgusts one.

The streets of the town are much too narrow for beauty or convenience—impracticable to coaches, and so beset with beggars that it is dreadful. A chair is therefore, above all things, necessary to be carried in, even a dozen steps, if you are likely to feel shocked at having your knees suddenly clasped by a figure hardly human, who, perhaps holding you forcibly for a minute, conjures you loudly by the sacred wounds of our Lord Jesus Christ to have compassion upon his, showing you at the same time such undeniable and horrid proofs of the anguish he is suffering that one must be a monster to quit him unrelieved. Such pathetic misery, such disgusting distress, did I never see before as I have been witness to in this gaudy city—and that not occasionally or by accident, but all day long, and in such numbers that humanity shrinks from the description. Sure, charity is not the virtue that they pray for when begging a blessing at the church-door.

One should not, however, speak unkindly of a people whose affectionate regard for our country showed itself so clearly during the late war. A few days' residence with the English consul here at his country seat gave me an opportunity of hearing many instances of the Republic's generous attachment to Great Britain, whose triumphs at Gibraltar over the united forces of France and Spain were honestly enjoyed by the friendly Genoese, who gave many proofs of their sincerity more solid than those clamorous ones of huzzaing our minister about wherever he went, and crying, 'Viva il General Elliott!' while many young gentlemen of high fashion offered themselves to go volunteers aboard our fleet, and were with difficulty restrained.

The sea-air, except in particular places where the land lies in some direction that counteracts its influence, is naturally inimical to timber, though the green coasts of Devonshire are finely fringed with wood, and here, at Lomellino's villa, in the Genoese State, I found two plane-trees of a size and serious dignity that recalled to my mind the solemn oak before our Duke of Dorset's seat at Knowle, and chestnuts which would not disgrace the forests of America. A rural theatre, cut in turf, with a concealed orchestra and sod-seats for the audience, with a mossy stage—not incommodious neither—and an admirable contrivancè for shifting the scenes and favouring the exits, entrances, etc., of the performers, gave me a perfect idea of that refined luxury which hot countries alone inspire—while another elegantly constructed spot, meant and often used for the entertainment of tenants and dependants who come to rejoice on the birth or wedding day of a kind landlord, make one suppress one's sighs after a free country—at least, suspend them—and fill one's heart with tenderness towards men who have skill to soften authority with indulgence, and virtue to reward obedience with protection.

A family coming last night to visit at a house where I had the honour of being admitted as an intimate, gave me another proof of my present state of remoteness from English manners. The party consisted of an old nobleman, who could trace his genealogy unblemished up to one of the old Roman emperors, but whose fortune is now in a hopeless state of decay; his lady, not inferior to himself in birth or haughtiness of air and carriage, but much impaired by age, ill-health, and pecuniary distresses. These had, however, no way lessened her ideas of her own dignity, or the respect of her cavalier servente and her son, who waited on her with an unremitted attention, presenting her their little dirty tin snuff-boxes upon one knee by turns, which ceremony the less surprised me, as having seen her train, made of a dyed and watered lutestring, borne gravely after her upstairs by a footman, the express image of Edgar in the storm scene of 'King Lear,' who, as the fool says, 'wisely reserv'd a blanket, else had we all been 'shamed.'

Our conversation was meagre, but serious. There was music, and the door being left at jar, as we call it, I watched the wretched servant who stayed in the antechamber, and found that he was listening in spite of sorrow and starving.

CHAPTER II

MILAN

Milan—Bad Weather—Distinctions of Rank—Household Management—Servants—Familiarity and Obsequiousness—Politeness—Roman Phrases—The Friars' Play—Christmas—Theatre of La Scala—Unaffected Manners—Snow—'Fossil Carbon'—The Corso—Paving—No Lady—Not a Gentleman—The Cavalier Servente—Filial Affection—Amiability towards Inferiors—Spiting the Archduke—Female Effrontery.

OUR weather is suddenly become so wet, the roads so heavy with incessant rain, that King William's departure from his own foggy country, or his welcome to our gloomy one, where this month is melancholy even to a proverb, could not have been clouded with a thicker atmosphere, surely, than was mine to Milan upon the fourth day of dismal November, 1784.

Italians, by what I can observe, suffer their minds to be much under the dominion of the sky, and attribute every change in their health, or even humour, as seriously to its influence as if there

were no nearer causes of alteration than the state of
the air, and as if no doubt remained of its immediate
power, though they are willing enough here to poison
it with the scent of wood-ashes within doors, while
fires in the grate seem to run rather low, and a
brazier full of that pernicious stuff is substituted in
its place, and driven under the table during dinner.
It is surprising how very elegant, not to say magnificent, those dinners are in gentlemen's or noblemen's
houses; such numbers of dishes at once—not large
joints, but infinite variety; and I think their cooking
excellent. Fashion keeps most of the fine people
out of town yet; we have therefore had leisure to
establish our own household for the winter, and
have done so as commodiously as if our habitation
was fixed here for life. This I am delighted with, as
one may chance to gain that insight into everyday
behaviour and common occurrences which can alone
be called knowing something of a country. Counting churches, pictures, palaces, may be done by
those who run from town to town, with no impression
made but on their bones.

Candour and a good-humoured willingness to
receive and reciprocate pleasure seems indeed one of
the standing virtues of Italy; I have as yet seen no
fastidious contempt or affected rejection of anything

for being what we call low, and I have a notion there is much less of those distinctions at Milan than at London, where birth does so little for a man, that if he depends on that and forbears other methods of distinguishing himself from his footman, he will stand a chance of being treated no better than him by the world. Here a person's rank is ascertained and his society settled at his immediate entrance into life; a gentleman and lady will always be regarded as such, let what will be their behaviour. It is, therefore, highly commendable when they seek to adorn their minds by culture, or pluck out those weeds which in hot countries will spring up among the riches of the harvest, and afford a sure but no immediately pleasing proof of the soil's natural fertility.

But my country-women would rather hear a little of our *interieur*, or, as we call it, family management, which appears arranged in a manner totally new to me, who find the lady of every house as unacquainted with her own and her husband's affairs as I who apply to her for information. No house account, no weekly bills perplex her peace. If eight servants are kept, we will say, six of these are men, and two of those men out of livery. The pay of these principal figures in the family, when at the highest rate, is fifteenpence English a day, out of which they find clothes and eating—for fifteenpence includes board-wages; and most of these fellows are married, too, and have four or five children each. The dinners dressed at home are, for this reason, more exactly contrived than in England to suit the number of guests, and there are always half a dozen; for dining alone, or the master and mistress *tête-à-tête*, as we do, is unknown to them, who make society very easy and resolve to live much together. No odd sensation, then, something like shame, such as we feel when too many dishes are taken empty from table, touches them at all. The common courses are eleven, and eleven small plates, and it is their sport and pleasure, if possible, to clear all away. A footman's wages is a shilling a day, like our common labourers, and paid him, as they are paid, every Saturday night. His livery, meantime, changed at least twice a year, makes him as rich a man as the butler and valet; but when evening comes, it is the comicallest sight in the world to see them all go gravely home, and you may die in the night for want of help, though surrounded by showy attendants all day. Till the hour of departure, however, it is expected that two or three of them at least sit in the antechamber, as it is called, to answer the bell, which, if we confess the truth, is no slight service or hardship; for the stairs, high and wide as those of Windsor Palace, all stone too, run up from the door immediately to that apartment, which is very large and very cold, with bricks to set their feet on only, and a brazier filled with warm wood-ashes to keep their fingers from freezing, which in summer they employ with cards, and seem but little inclined to lay them down when ladies pass through to the receiving-room. The strange familiarity this class of people think proper to assume, half-joining in the conversation, and crying ' Oibò !'* when the master affirms something they do not quite assent to, is apt to shock one at beginning, the more when one reflects upon the equally offensive humility they show on being first accepted into the family, when it is expected that they receive the new master's or lady's hand in a half-kneeling posture and kiss it, as women under the rank of countess do the Queen of England's when presented at our court. This obsequiousness, however, vanishes completely upon acquaintance, and the footman, if not very seriously admonished indeed, yawns, spits, and displays what one of our travel-writers emphatically terms his flag of abomination behind the chair of a woman of quality without the slightest sensation of its impropriety. There is, however, a sort of odd farcical drollery mingled with this gross-

* ' Oh, dear !'

ness, which tends greatly to disarm one's wrath; and I felt more inclined to laugh than be angry one day, when, from the head of my own table, I saw the servant of a nobleman who dined with us cramming some chicken patés down his throat behind the door, our own folks humorously trying to choke him by pretending that his lord called him while his mouth was full. Of a thousand comical things in the same way, I will relate one. Mr. Piozzi's valet was dressing my hair at Paris one morning, while some man sat at an opposite window of the same inn, singing and playing upon the violoncello. I had not observed the circumstance, but my perrucchiere's distress was evident; he writhed and twisted about like a man pinched with the colic, and pulled a hundred queer faces. At last:

'What is the matter, Ercolani?' said I. 'Are you not well?'

'Mistress,' replies the fellow, 'if that beast don't leave off soon, I shall run mad with rage, or else die; and so you'll see an honest Venetian lad killed by a French dog's howling.'

The phrase of mistress is here not confined to servants at all; gentlemen, when they address one, cry 'Mia padrona'* mighty sweetly, and in a pecu-

* My mistress.

liarly pleasing tone. Nothing, to speak truth, can exceed the agreeableness of a well-bred Italian's address when speaking to a lady, whom they alone know how to flatter so as to retain her dignity and not lose their own—respectful, yet tender; attentive, not officious. The politeness of a man of fashion here is true politeness, free from all affectation, and honestly expressive of what he really feels—a true value for the person spoken to, without the smallest desire of shining himself—equally removed from foppery on one side or indifference on the other. The manners of the men here are certainly pleasing to a very eminent degree, and in their conversation there is a mixture—not unfrequent, too— of classical allusions, which strike one with a sort of literary pleasure I cannot easily describe. Yet is there no pedantry in their use of expressions which with us would be laughable or liable to censure; but Roman notions here are not quite extinct, and even the housemaid, or donna di gros, as they call her, swears by Diana so comically, there is no telling. They christen their boys Fabius, their daughters Claudia, very commonly. When they mention a thing known, as we say, to Tom o' Styles and John o' Nokes, they use the words Tizio and Sempronio. A lady tells me she was at a loss about the dance yesterday evening, because she had not been instructed in the programma; and a gentleman, talking of the pleasures he enjoyed supping last night at a friend's house, exclaims, 'Eramo pur seri fera in Appolline!'* alluding to Lucullus's entertainment given to Pompey and Cicero, as I remember, in the chamber of Apollo. But here is enough of this—more of it, in their own pretty phrase, seccarebbe pur Nettunno.† It was long ago that Ausonius said of them more than I can say, and Mr. Addison has translated the lines in their praise better than I could have done:

> 'Et Mediolani mira omnia copia rerum :
> Innumeræ cultæque domus facunda virorum
> Ingenia et mores læti.'

> 'Milan with plenty and with wealth o'erflows,
> And numerous streets and cleanly dwellings shows;
> The people, bless'd by Nature's happy force,
> Are eloquent and cheerful in discourse.'

What I have said this moment will, however, account in some measure for a thing which he treats with infinite contempt, not unjustly perhaps; yet does it not deserve the ridicule handed down from his time by all who have touched the subject. It is about the author, who before his theatrical representation prefixes an odd declaration, that though he names Pluto and Neptune, and I know not who,

* 'We passed yester evening as if we had been in the Apollo.'
† 'Would dry up old Neptune himself.'

upon the stage, yet he believes none of those fables, but considers himself as a Christian, a Catholic, etc. All this does appear very absurdly superfluous to us; but, as I observed, they live nearer the original seats of paganism; many old customs are yet retained, and the names not lost among them, or laid up merely for literary purposes as in England. They swear per Bacco perpetually in common discourse, and once I saw a gentleman in the heat of conversation blush at the recollection that he had said 'barba Jove' where he meant God Almighty.

By the indulgence of private friendship, I have now enjoyed the uncommon amusement of seeing a theatrical exhibition performed by friars in a convent for their own diversion and that of some select friends. The monks of St. Victor had, it seems, obtained permission this carnival to represent a little odd sort of play, written by one of their community chiefly in the Milanese dialect, though the upper characters spoke Tuscan. The subject of this drama was taken, naturally enough, from some events, real or fictitious, which were supposed to have happened in the environs of Milan about a hundred years ago, when the Torriani and Visconti families disputed for superiority. Its construction was compounded of comic and distressful scenes, of which the last gave me most delight ; and much was I amazed, indeed, to feel my cheeks wet with tears at a friar's play, founded on ideas of parental tenderness. The comic part, however, was intolerably gross; the jokes coarse, and incapable of diverting any but babies, or men who, by a kind of intellectual privation, contrive to perpetuate babyhood in the vain hope of preserving innocence; nor could I flatter myself by saying how little I understood of the dialect it was written in, as the action was nothing less than equivocal; and in the burletta which was tacked to it by way of farce, I saw the soprano singers who played the women's parts, and who see more of the world than these friars, blush for shame two or three times, while the company, most of them grave ecclesiastics, applauded with rapturous delight.

The wearisome length of the whole would, however, have surfeited me, had the amusement been more eligible ; but these dear monks do not get a holiday often, I trust ; so in the manner of schoolboys, or, rather, school-girls in England (for our boys are soon above such stuff), they were never tired of this dull buffoonery, and kept us listening to it till one o'clock in the morning.

Pleasure, when it does come, always bursts up in an unexpected place ; I derived much from observing in the faces of these cheerful friars that intelligent shrewdness and arch penetration so visible in the countenances of our Welsh farmers and curates of country villages in Flintshire, Carnarvonshire, etc., which Howel (best judge in such a case) observes in his Letters, and learnedly accounts for, but which I had wholly forgotten till the monks of St. Victor brought it back to my remembrance.

The brothers who remained unemployed and clear from stage occupations formed the orchestra; those who were left then without any immediate business upon their hands chatted gaily with the company, producing plenty of refreshments; and I was really very angry with myself for feeling so cynically disposed, when everything possible was done to please me.

The Christmas functions here were showy and, I thought, well contrived—the public ones are what I speak of; but I was present lately at a private merry-making, where all distinctions seemed pleasingly thrown down by a spirit of innocent gaiety. The marquis's daughter mingled in country-dances with the apothecary's apprentice, while her truly noble parents looked on with generous pleasure and encouraged the mirth of the moment. Priests, ladies, gentlemen of the very first quality, romped with the girls of the house in high good-humour, and tripped it away without the encumbrance of petty pride, or the mean vanity of giving what they expressively call 'soggezzione' to those who were proud of their company and protection. A new-married wench, whose little fortune of a hundred crowns had been given her by the subscription of many in the room, seemed as free with them all as the most equal distribution of birth or riches could have made her; she laughed aloud and rattled in the ears of the gentlemen, replied with sarcastic coarseness when they joked her, and apparently delighted to promote such conversation as they would not otherwise have tried at. The ladies shouted for joy, encouraged the girl with less delicacy than desire of merriment, and promoted a general banishment of decorum, though I do believe with full as much or more purity of intention than may be often met with in a polished circle at Paris itself.

Such society, however, can please a stranger only as it is odd and as it is new; when ceremony ceases, hilarity is left in a state too natural not to offend people accustomed to scenes of high civilization, and I suppose few of us could return, after twenty-five years old, to the coarse comforts of a roll and treacle.

Another style of amusement, very different from

this last, called us out two or three days ago—to hear the famous 'Passione' of Metastasio sung in St. Celso's Church. The building is spacious, the architecture elegant, and the ornaments rich. A custom, too, was on this occasion omitted, which I dislike exceedingly—that of deforming the beautiful edifices dedicated to God's service with damask hangings and gold lace on the capitals of all the pillars upon days of gala, so very perversely that the effect of proportions is lost to the eye, while the church conveys no idea to the mind but of a tattered theatre; and when the frippery decorations fade, nothing can exclude the recollection of an old clothes' shop. St. Celso was, however, left clear from these disgraceful ornaments; there assembled together a numerous and brilliant, if not an attentive, audience; and St. Peter's part in the oratorio was sung by a soprano voice, with no appearance of peculiar propriety, to be sure.

It is now time to talk a little of the theatre, and surely a receptacle so capacious to contain four thousand people, a place of entrance so commodious to receive them, a show so princely, so very magnificent to entertain them, must be sought in vain out of Italy. The centre front box, richly adorned with gilding, arms and trophies, is appropriated to the court, whose canopy is carried up to what we call the first gallery in England; the crescent of boxes ending with the stage consists of nineteen on a side, small boudoirs—for such they seem—and are as such fitted up with silk hangings, girandoles, etc., and placed so judiciously as to catch every sound of the singers if they do but whisper. I will not say it is equally advantageous to the figure as to the voice, no performers looking adequate to the place they recite upon, so very stately is the building itself, being all of stone, with an immense portico, and stairs which for width you might without hyperbole drive your chariot up. An immense sideboard at the first lobby, lighted and furnished with luxurious and elegant plenty, as many people send for suppers to their box and entertain a knot of friends there with infinite convenience and splendour. A silk curtain, the colour of your hangings, defends the closet from intrusive eyes, if you think proper to drop it, and, when drawn up, gives gaiety and show to the general appearance of the whole; while across the corridor leading to these boxes another small chamber, numbered like that it belongs to, is appropriated to the use of your servants, and furnished with every conveniency to make chocolate, serve lemonade, etc.

Can one wonder at the contempt shown by

foreigners when they see English women of fashion squeezed into holes lined with dirty, torn red paper, and the walls of it covered with a wretched crimson stuff? Well, but this theatre is built in place of a church, founded by the famous Beatrice di Scala, in consequence of a vow she made to erect one if God would be pleased to send her a son. The church was pulled down and the playhouse erected. The Archduke lost a son that year, and the pious folks cried, 'A judgment!' but nobody minded them, I believe; many, however, that are scrupulous will not go. Meantime, it is a beautiful theatre, to be sure—the finest fabric raised in modern days, I do believe, for the purposes of entertainment; but we must not be partial. While London has twelve capital rooms for the professed amusement of the public, Milan has but one; there is in it, however, a ridotto chamber for cards of a noble size, where some little gaming goes on in carnival time; but, though the inhabitants complain of the enormities committed there, I suppose more money is lost and won at one club in St. James's Street during a week than here at Milan in the whole winter.

That neither complaints nor rejoicings here at Milan proceed from affectation is a choice comfort; the Lombards possess the skill to please you without feigning, and, so artless are their manners, you cannot even suspect them of insincerity. They have, perhaps for that very reason, few comedies and fewer novels among them, for the worst of every man's character is already well known to the rest; but be his conduct what it will, the heart is commonly right enough—'il buon cuor Lombardo' is famed throughout all Italy, and nothing can become proverbial without an excellent reason. Little opportunity is, therefore, given to writers who carry the dark lantern of life into its deepest recesses—unwind the hidden wickedness of a Maskwell or a Monkton, develop the folds of vice, and spy out the internal worthlessness of apparent virtue, which from these discerning eyes cannot be cloaked even by the early-taught affectation which renders it a real ingenuity to discover if in a highly-polished capital a man or woman has or has not good parts or principles—so completely are the first overlaid with literature and the last perverted by refinement.

April 2, 1785.

The cold weather continues still, and we have heavy snows; but so admirable is the police of this well-regulated town, that when over-night it has fallen to the height of four feet—no very uncommon occurrence—no one can see in the morning that even a flake has been there, so completely do the poor and the prisoners rid us of it all by throwing immense loads of it into a navigable canal that runs quite round the city and carries every nuisance with it clearly away, so that no inconveniences can arise.

Italians seem to me to have no feeling of cold; they open the casements—for windows we have none—now in winter, and cry, 'Che bel freschetto!'* while I am starving outright. If there is a flash of a few faggots in the chimney that just scorches one a little, no lady goes near it, but sits at the other end of a high-roofed room, the wind whistling round her ears, and her feet upon a perforated brass box filled with wood-embers, which the cavalier servente pulls out from time to time and replenishes with hotter ashes raked out from between the andirons. How sitting with these fumes under their petticoats improves their beauty of complexion I know not; certain it is they pity us exceedingly for our manner of managing ourselves, and inquire of their countrymen who have lived here awhile how their health endured the burning fossils in the chambers at London. I have heard two or three Italians say, 'Vorrei anch' io veder quell' Inghilterra, ma questo

* 'What a fresh breeze!'

carbone fossile!'* To church, however, and to the theatre, ladies have a great green velvet bag carried for them, adorned with gold tassels and lined with fur, to keep their feet from freezing, as carpets are not in use here. Poor women run about the streets with a little earthen pipkin hanging on their arm filled with fire, even if they are sent on an errand; while men of all ranks walk wrapped up in an odd sort of white riding-coat, not buttoned together, but folded round their body after the fashion of the old Roman dress that one has seen in statues, and this they call 'gaban,' retaining many Spanish words since the time that they were under Spanish government. Buscar, 'to seek,' is quite familiar here as at Madrid, and instead of Ragazzo, I have heard the Milanese say 'Mozzo di Stalla,' which is originally a Castilian word, I believe, and spelt by them with the *c* con cedilla, Moço. They have likewise Latin phrases oddly mingled among their own. A gentleman said yesterday that he was going to Casa Sororis, to his sister's; and the strange word, minga, which meets one at every turn, is corrupted, I believe, from mica, 'a crumb.' 'Piaz minga,' 'I have not a crumb of pleasure in it,' etc.

The uniformity of dress here pleases the eye, and

---

* 'I would go see this same England myself, I think, but that fuel made of minerals frights me.'

their custom of going veiled to church, and always without a hat, which they consider as profanation of the temple, as they call it, delights me much; it has an air of decency in the individuals, of general respect for the place, and of a resolution not to let external images intrude on devout thoughts. The hanging churches, and even public pillars set up in the streets or squares for purposes of adoration, with black when any person of consequence dies, displeases me more; it is so very dismal, so paltry a piece of pride and expiring vanity, and so dirty a custom—calling bugs and spiders and all manner of vermin about one so in those black trappings—it is terrible; but if they remind us of our end, and set us about preparing for it, the benefit is greater than the evil.

The equipages on the Corso here are very numerous, in proportion to the size of the city, and excessively showy; the horses are long-tailed, heavy, and for the most part black, with high-rising forehands, while the sinking of the back is artfully concealed by the harness of red morocco leather richly ornamented, and white reins. To this magnificence much is added by large leopard, panther, or tiger skins, beautifully striped or spotted by Nature's hand, and held fast on the horses by heavy, shining tassels of gold, coloured lace, etc., wonderfully handsome;

while the driver, clothed in a bright scarlet dress, adorned and trimmed with bear's-skin, makes a noble figure on the box at this season upon days of gala. The carnival, however, exhibits a variety unspeakable; boats and barges painted of a thousand colours, drawn upon wheels, and filled with masks and merrymakers, who throw sugar-plums at each other, to the infinite delight of the town, whose populousness that show evinces to perfection; for every window and balcony is crowded to excess, the streets are fuller than one can express of gazers, and general mirth and gaiety prevail. When the flashing season is over, and you are no longer to be dazzled with finery or stunned with noise, the nobility of Milan—for gentry there are none—fairly slip a check case over the hammock, as we do to our best chairs in England, clap a coarse leather cover on the carriage-top, the coachman wearing a vast brown greatcoat, which he spreads on each side of him over the corners of his coach-box, and looks, as somebody was saying, like a sitting hen.

The paving of our streets here at Milan is worth mentioning, only because it is directly contrary to the London method of performing the same operation. They lay the large flagstones at this place in two rows for the coach-wheels to roll smoothly over, leaving walkers to accommodate themselves and bear the sharp pebbles to their tread as they may. In everything great and everything little, the diversity of government must perpetually occur; where that is despotic, small care will be taken of the common people; where that is popular, little attention will be paid to the great ones. I never in my whole life heard so much of birth and family as since I came to this town—where blood enjoys a thousand exclusive privileges; where Cavalier and Dama are words of the first, nay, of the only importance; where wit and beauty are considered as useless without a long pedigree, and virtue, talents, wealth, and wisdom are thought on only as medals to hang upon the branch of a genealogical tree, as we tie trinkets to a watch in England.

I went to church, twenty yards from our own door, with a servant to wait on me, three or four mornings ago; there was a lady, particularly well-dressed, very handsome, two footmen attending on her at a distance, took my attention.

'Peter,' said I to my own man, as we came out, 'chi è quella dama?' (who is that lady?)

'Non è dama' (she is no lady), replies the fellow, contemptuously smiling at my simplicity.

I thought she might be somebody's kept mistress, and asked him whose.

'Dio ne liberi!' (God forbid!) returns Peter, in a

kinder accent—for there heart came in, and he would not injure her character; 'è moglie d'un ricco banchiere' (she is a rich banker's wife). 'You may see,' added he, 'that she is no lady if you look. The servants carry no velvet stool for her to kneel upon, and they have no coat armour in the lace to their liveries. *She* a lady!' repeated he again, with infinite contempt.

I am told that the Archduke is very desirous to close this breach of distinction, and to draw merchants and traders, with their wives, up into higher notice than they were wont to remain in. I do not think he will by that means conciliate the affection of any rank. The prejudices in favour of nobility are too strong to be shaken here, much less rooted out so; the very servants would rather starve in the house of a man of family than eat after a person of inferior quality, whom they consider as their equal and almost treat him as such to his face. Shall we, then, be able to refuse our particular veneration to those characters of high rank here who add the charm of a cultivated mind to that situation which, united even with ignorance, would ensure them respect? When scholarship is found among the great in Italy, it has the additional merit of having grown up in their own bosoms, without encouragement from emulation or the least interested motive.

His companions do not think much the more of him for that kind of superiority. 'I suppose,' says a friend of his, 'he must be fond of study; for chi pensa d' una maniera, chi pensa d'un' altra, per me sono stato sempre ignorantissimo.'*

These voluntary confessions of many a quality, which, whether possessed or not by English people, would certainly never be avowed, spring from that native sincerity I have been praising, for, though family connections are prized so highly here, no man seems ashamed that he has no family to boast: all feigning would, indeed, be useless and impracticable; yet it struck me with astonishment, too, to hear a well-bred clergyman, who visits at many genteel houses, say gravely to his friend, no longer ago than yesterday—that friend a man, too, eminent both for talents and fortune:

'Yes, there is a grand invitation at such a place to-night, but I don't go because I am not a gentleman—perche non sono cavaliere; and the master desired I would let you know that it was for no other reason that you had not a card too, my good friend; for it is an invitation of none but people of fashion, you see.'

At all this nobody stares, nobody laughs, and

---

* 'One man is of one mind, another of another; I was always a sheer dunce for my own part.'

nobody's throat is cut in consequence of their sincere declarations.

The women are not behindhand in openness of confidence and comical sincerity. We have all heard much of Italian cicisbeism; I had a mind to know how matters really stood, and took the nearest way to information by asking a mighty beautiful and apparently artless young creature, not noble, how that affair was managed—'for there is no harm done, I am sure,' said I.

'Why, no,' replied she—'no great harm, to be sure, except wearisome attentions from a man one cares little about. For my own part,' continued she, 'I detest the custom, as I happen to love my husband excessively, and desire nobody's company in the world but his. We are not people of fashion though, you know, nor at all rich; so how should we set fashions for our betters? They would only say, "See how jealous he is," if Mr. Such-a-one sat much with me at home, or went with me to the Corso; and I must go with some gentleman, you know. And the men are such ungenerous creatures, and have such ways with them. I want money often, and this cavaliere servente pays the bills, and so the connection draws closer—that's all.'

'And your husband?' said I.

'Oh, why, he likes to see me well-dressed. He is

very good-natured and very charming; I love him to my heart.'

' And your confessor?' cried I.

' Oh, why, he is used to it'—in the Milanese dialect, ' è assuefaà.'

The mind of an Italian, whether man or woman, seldom fails, for aught I see, to make up in extent what is wanted in cultivation; and that they possess the art of pleasing in an eminent degree, the constancy with which they are mutually beloved by each other is the best proof.

Ladies of distinction bring with them when they marry, besides fortune, as many clothes as will last them seven years; for fashions do not change here as often as at London or Paris; yet is pin-money allowed, and an attention paid to the wife that no English woman can form an idea of. In every family her duties are few, for, as I have observed, household management falls to the master's share of course, when all the servants are men almost, and those all paid by the week or day. Children are very seldom seen by those who visit great houses; if they do come down for five minutes after dinner, the parents are talked of as doating on them, and nothing can equal the pious and tender return made to fathers and mothers in this country for even an apparently moderate share of fondness shown to them in a state of infancy. I saw an old marchioness the other day, who had, I believe, been exquisitely beautiful, lying in bed in a spacious apartment, just like ours in the old palaces, with the tester touching the top almost; she had her three grown-up sons standing round her, with an affectionate desire of pleasing and showing her whatever could soothe or amuse her, so that it charmed me; and I was told —and observed, indeed—that when they quitted her presence, a half-kneeling bow and a kind kiss of her still white hand was the ceremony used. I knew myself brought thither only that she might be entertained with the sight of the foreigner, and was equally struck at her appearance—more so, I should imagine, than she could be at mine—when these dear men assisted in moving her pillows with emulative attention and rejoiced with each other apart that their mother looked so well to-day. Two or three servants out of livery brought us refreshments, I remember; but her maid attended in the antechamber and answered the bell at her bed's-head, which was exceedingly magnificent in the old style of grandeur—crimson damask, if I recollect right, with family arms at the back; and she lay on nine or eleven pillows, laced with ribbon, and two large bows to each, very elegant and expensive in any

A LADY SPINNING.
After Pietro Longhi.

country. With all this, to prove that the Italians have little sensation of cold, here was no fire, but a suffocating brazier, which stood near the door that opened, and was kept open, into the maid's apartment.

A woman here in every stage of life has really a degree of attention shown her that is surprising. If conjugal disputes arise in a family, so as to make them become what we call town-talk, the public voice is sure to run against the husband; if separation ensues, all possible countenance is given to the wife, while the gentleman is somewhat less willingly received, and all the stories of past disgusts are related to his prejudice, nor will the lady whom he wishes to serve look very kindly on a man who treats his own wife with unpoliteness. 'Che cuore deve avere!' (What a heart he must have!) says she. 'Io non mene fido sicuro' (I shall take care not to trust him, sure).

National character is a great matter. I did not know there had been such a difference in the ways of thinking, merely from custom and climate, as I see there is, though one has always read of it. It was, however, entertaining enough to hear a travelled gentleman haranguing away three nights ago at our house in praise of English cleanliness, and telling his auditors how all the men in London that were noble put on a clean shirt every day, and the women washed the street before his house-door every morning.

'Che schiavitù mai!' exclaimed a lady of quality, who was listening; 'ma naturalmente sarà per commando del principe.' 'What a land of slavery!' says Donna Louisa—I heard her; 'but it is all done by command of the sovereign, I suppose.'

Their ideas of justice are no less singular than of delicacy, but those are more easily accounted for; so is their amiable carriage towards inferiors, calling their own and their friends' servants by tender names, and speaking to all below themselves with a graciousness not often used by English men or women even to their equals. The pleasure, too, which the high people here express when the low ones are diverted is charming. We think it vulgar to be merry when the mob is so; but if rolling down a hill, like Greenwich, was the custom here as with us, all Milan would run to see the sport, and rejoice in the felicity of their fellow-creatures. When I express my admiration of such condescending sweetness, they reply, 'È un uomo come un altro; è battezzato come noi,' and the like—'Why, he is a man of the same nature as we; he has been christened as well as ourselves,' they reply. Yet do I not for this reason condemn the English as naturally haughty above their continental neighbours. Our Government has left so narrow a space between the upper and under ranks of people in Great Britain, while our charitable and truly Christian religion is still so constantly employed in raising the depressed by giving them means of changing their situation, that if our persons of condition fail even for a moment to watch their post, maintaining by dignity what they or their fathers have acquired by merit, they are instantly and suddenly broken in upon by the well-employed talents or swiftly acquired riches of men born on the other side the thin partition; whilst in Italy the gulf is totally impassable, and birth alone can entitle man or woman to the society of gentlemen and ladies. This firmly-fixed idea of subordination (which I once heard a Venetian say he believed must exist in heaven from one angel to another) accounts immediately for a little conversation which I am now going to relate.

Here were two men taken up last week, one for murdering his fellow-servant in cold blood, while the undefended creature had the lemonade tray in his hand going in to serve company; the other for breaking the new lamps lately set up with intention to light this town in the manner of the streets at Paris.

'I hope,' said I, 'they will hang the murderer.'

'I rather hope,' replied a very sensible lady who sat near me, 'that they will hang the person who broke the lamps; for,' added she, 'the first committed his crime only out of revenge, poor fellow! because the other had got his mistress from him by treachery; but this creature has had the impudence to break our fine new lamps, all for the sake of spiting the Archduke.'

The Archduke, meantime, hangs nobody at all, but sets his prisoners to work upon the roads, public buildings, etc., where they labour in their chains, and where—strange to tell—they often insult passengers who refuse them alms when asked as they go by, and—stranger still—they are not punished for it when they do.

Here is certainly much despotic power in Italy, but, I fancy, very little oppression; perhaps authority, once acknowledged, does not delight itself always by the fatigue of exertion. 'Sat est prostrasse leoni' is an old adage, with which perhaps I may be the better acquainted, as it is the motto to my own coat-of-arms; and unless sovereignty is hungry, for aught I see, he does not certainly devour.

The certainty of their irrevocable doom, softened by kind usage from their superiors, makes, in the meantime, an odd sort of humorous drollery spring up among the common people, who are much happier here at Milan than I expected to find them, every great house giving meat, broth, etc., to poor dependents with liberal good-nature enough, so that mighty little wandering misery is seen in the streets; unlike those of Genoa, who seem mocked with the word liberty, while sorrow, sickness, and the most pinching want pine at the doors of marble palaces, whose owners are unfeeling as their walls.

Our ordinary people here in Lombardy are well-clothed, fat, stout and merry, and desirous to divert themselves and their protectors, whom they love at their hearts. There is, however, a degree of effrontery among the women that amazes me, and of which I had no idea, till a friend showed me one evening, from my own box at the opera, fifty or a hundred low shopkeepers' wives, dispersed about the pit at the theatre, dressed in men's clothes— 'per disimpegno,' as they call it—that they might be more at liberty forsooth to clap and hiss, and quarrel and jostle, etc. I felt shocked.

'One who comes from a free government need not wonder so,' said he.

'On the contrary, sir,' replied I, 'where everybody has hopes—at least, possibility—of bettering his station and advancing nearer to the limits of upper life, none except the most abandoned of their species will wholly lose sight of such decorous conduct as alone can grace them when they have reached their wish : whereas your people know their destiny, future as well as present, and think no more of deserving a higher post than they think of obtaining it.'

CHAPTER III

MANTUA, VERONA, AND PADUA

Lodi — Ballet of 'Don Juan' — Mantua — Concert — Ladies' Dress — Verona — A Bull-fight in the Amphitheatre — Amusements — A Heretic's Burial — Padua — Horror of Suicide — A Poor Astronomer — The Sweet Paduans.

Lodi.

THE first evening's drive carried us no farther than Lodi, a place renowned through all Europe for its excellent cheese, as our well-known ballad bears testimony:

'Let Lodi or Parmesan bring up the rear.'

The town, however, bringing no other ideas either new or old to our minds, we went to the opera and heard Morichelli sing, after which they gave us a new dramatic dance, made upon the story of 'Don John; or, The Libertine,' a tale which, whether true or false, fact or fable, has furnished every Christian country in the world, I believe, with some subject of representation. It makes me no sport, however; the idea of an impenitent sinner going to hell is too seriously terrifying to make amusement out of. Let mythology, which is now grown good for little else, be danced upon the stage, where Mr. Vestris may bounce and struggle in the character of Alcides on his funeral pile with no very glaring impropriety; and such baubles serve beside to keep old classical stories in the heads of our young people, who, if they must have torches to blaze in their eyes, may divert themselves with Pluto catching up Ceres' daughter and driving her away to Tartarus; but let Don John alone. I have at least half a notion that the horrible history is half true; if so, it is surely very gross to represent it by dancing. Should such false, foolish taste prevail in England (but I hope it will not), we might perhaps go happily through the whole book of 'God's Revenge against Murder,' or the 'Annals of Newgate,' on the stage.

Mantua.

The theatres here are beautiful beyond all telling; it is a shame not to take the model of the small one and build a place of entertainment on the plan. There cannot surely be any plan more elegant.

We had a concert of admirable music at the house of our new acquaintance in the evening, and were introduced by his means to many people of fashion.

The ladies were pretty and dressed with much taste —no caps at all, but flowers in their heads, and earrings of silver filigree finely worked, long, light and thin. I never saw such before, but it would be an exceeding pretty fashion. They hung down quite low upon the neck and shoulders, and had a pleasing effect.

Verona, April 10.

How beautiful the entrance is of this charming city, how grand the gate, how handsome the drive forward, may all be read here in a printed book called 'Verona Illustrata'; but my felicity in finding the amphitheatre so well preserved can only be found in my own heart, which began sensibly to dilate at the seeing an old Roman coliseum kept so nicely and repaired so well.

A bull-feast given here to divert the Emperor as he passed through must have excited many pleasing sensations, while the inhabitants sat on seats once occupied by the masters of the world, and, what is more worth wonder, sat at the feet of a Transalpine Cæsar, for so the sovereign of Germany is even now called by his Milanese subjects in common discourse; and when one looks upon the arms of Austria, a spread-eagle, and recollects that when the Roman empire was divided the old eagle was split, one face looking toward the east, the other toward the west, in token of shared possession, it affects one, and calls up classic imagery to the mind.

The collection of antiquities belonging to the Philharmonic Society is very respectable; they reminded me of the Arundel marbles at Oxford, and I said so.

'Oh,' replied the man who showed these, 'that collection was very valuable, to be sure; but the bad air and the smoke of coal-fires in England have ruined them long ago.'

I suspected that my gentleman talked by rote, and, examining the book called 'Verona Illustrata,' found the remark there; but this is 'malafede,' and a very ridiculous prejudice.

'A Verona mezzi matti,'* say the Italians themselves of them, and I see nothing seemingly go forward here but improvisatori, reciting stories or verses to entertain the populace; boys flying kites, cut square like a diamond on the cards, and called Stelle; men amusing themselves at a game called pallamajo, something like our cricket, only that they throw the ball with a hollow stick, not with the hand, but it requires no small corporal strength. And I know not why our English people have such a

* 'The people at Verona are half out of their wits.'

notion of Italian effeminacy; games of very strong exertion are in use among them, and I have not yet felt one hot day since I left France.

They showed us an agreeable garden here, belonging to some man of fashion whose name I know not; it was cut in a rock, yet the grotto disappointed me. They had not taken such advantages of the situation as Lomellino would have done, and I recollected the tasteful creations in my own country—Pain's Hill and Stour Head.

The Veronese nobleman showed, however, the spirit of his country, if we let loose the genius of ours. The emperor had visited his improvements, it seems, and on the spot where he kissed the children of the house their father set up a stone to record the honour.

Our attendant related a tender story, to me more interesting, which happened in this garden, of an English gentleman who, having hired the house, etc., one season, found his favourite servant ill there, and like to die. The poor creature expressed his concern at the intolerant cruelty of that sect which denies Christians of any other denomination but their own a place in consecrated ground, and lamented his distance from home with an anxious earnestness that hastened his end, when the humanity of his master sent him to the landlord, who kindly gave permission that he might lie undisturbed under his turf, as one places one's lapdog in England; and there, as our *laquais de place* observed, he did no harm, though he was a heretic, and the English gentleman wept over his grave.

Our equipages here are strangely inferior to those we left behind at Milan. Oil is burned in the conversation rooms, too, and smells very offensively; but they lament our 'suffocation in England, and black smoke,' while what proceeds from these lamps would ruin the finest furniture in the world before five weeks were expired. I saw no such used at Turin, Genoa, or Milan.

The horses here are not equal to those I have admired on the Corso at other great towns, but it is pleasing to observe the contrast between the high-bred, airy, elegant English hunter and the majestic, docile and well-broken war-horse of Lombardy. Shall we fancy there is Gothic and Grecian to be found even among the animals? or is not that too fanciful?

Before leaving the plains of Lombardy, I will give my country-women one reason for detaining them so long there. It cannot be an uninteresting reason to us, when we reflect that our first head-dresses were made by Milaners; that a court-gown was early known in England by the name of a mantua, from Manto, the daughter of Teresias, who founded the city so called; and that some of the best materials for making these mantuas is still named from the town it is manufactured in—a Padua soy.

Padua.

Padua la dotta afforded me much pleasure, from the politeness of the Countess Ferres, born a German, of the house of Starenberg. She thought proper to show me a thousand civilities, in consequence of a kind letter which we carried her from Count Wiltseck, the Austrian minister at Milan—called the literati of the town about us, and gave me the pleasure of conversing with the Abate Cesarotti, who translated 'Ossian,' and the Professor Statico, whose attentions I ought never to forget. I was surprised at length to hear kind inquiries after English acquaintance made in my native language by the botanical professor, who spoke much of Dr. Johnson, and with great regard. He had, it seems, spent much time in our island about thirty years before.

The debtor's stone in the hall of justice has many entertaining stories annexed to it. The bankrupt is obliged to sit there in presence of his creditors and judges in a very disgraceful state, and many accounts are told one of the various effects such distresses have had on the mind; but suicide is a crime rarely committed out of England, and the Italians look with just horror on our people for being so easily incited to a sin which takes from him that commits it all power and possibility of repentance.

A Frenchman, whom I sent for once at Bath to dress my hair, gave me an excellent trait of his own national character, speaking upon that subject, when he meant to satirize ours.

'You have lived some years in England, friend,' said I; 'do you like it?'

'Mais non, madame, pas parfaitement bien.'*

'You have travelled much in Italy. Do you like that better?'

'Ah, Dieu ne plaise, madame, je n'aime guère messieurs les Italiens.'†

'What do they do to make you hate them so?'

'Mais c'est que les Italiens se tuent l'un l'autre,' replied the fellow, 'et les Anglais se font un plaisir de se tuer eux-mêmes: pardi je ne me sens rien moins qu'un vrai gout pour ces gentillesses là, et j'aimerais mieux me trouver à Paris, pour rire un peu.'‡

---

* 'Why, no truly, ma'am, not much.'

† 'Oh, God forbid!—no, I cannot endure those Italians.'

‡ 'Why, really, the Italians have such a passion for murdering each ther, ma'am, and the English such an odd delight in killing them-

Besides the civilities shown us here by Mr. Bonaldi and his agreeable lady, Signora Annetta, we were recommended by letters from the Venetian resident at Milan to Abate Toaldo, professor of astronomy, who wished to do all in his power to oblige and entertain us. His observatory is a good one; but the learned, amiable scholar, who resides in the first-floor of it, complained to us that he was sickly, old and poor—three bad qualifications, as he observed, for the amusement of travellers, who commonly arrive hungry for novelty and thirsty for information. His quadrant was very fine — the planetarium, or orrery, quite out of repair, and his references, of course, were obliged to be made to a sort of map or chart of the heavenly bodies (a solar system, at least, with comets) that hung up in his room as a substitute. He had little reverence for the petrefactions of Monte Bolca, I perceived, which he considered as mere *lusus naturæ*. He showed me poor Petrarch's tomb from his observatory, bid me look on Sir Isaac's full-length picture in the room, and said the world would see no more such men. Of our Maskelyne, however, no man could speak with more esteem or expressions of

---

selves, that I, who have acquired no taste for such agreeable amusements, grow somewhat impatient to return to Paris and get a good laugh among my old acquaintance.'

generous friendship. His sitting-chamber was a pleasant one, and I should not have left it so soon but in compassion to his health, which our company was more likely to injure than assist. He asked me if I did not find 'Padua la dotta' a very stinking, nasty town, but added that literature and dirt had long been intimately acquainted, and that this city was commonly called among the Italians ' Porcil de Padua '—' Padua the Pig-sty.'

I must not leave the *terra firma*, as they call it, without mentioning once more some of the animals it produces, among which the asses are so justly renowned for their size and beauty, that 'Come un asino di Padua' is proverbial when speaking of strength among the Italians. How should it be otherwise, indeed, where every herb and every shrub breathes fragrance, and where the quantity, as well as the quality, of their food naturally so increases their milk, that I should think some of them might yield as much as an ordinary cow?

This town, as Abbé Toaldo observed, is old and dirty and melancholy-looking in itself; but Terence told us long ago, and truly, 'that it was not the walls, but the company, made every place delightful,' and these inhabitants, though few in number, are so exceedingly cheerful, so charming, their language is so mellifluous, their manners so soothing, I can scarcely bear to leave them without tears.

Verona was the first place I felt reluctance to quit, but the Venetian state certainly possesses uncommon, and to me almost unaccountable, attractions. Be that as it will, we leave these sweet Paduans tomorrow. The coach is disposed of, and we are to set out upon our watery journey to their wonderfully-situated metropolis, or, as they call it prettily,' La Bella Dominante.

CHAPTER IV

VENICE

St. Mark's Place—Decorations—The Republic—Venice at Night—A Lady's Way into a Monastery—The Rialto—Gondoliers—A Female Orchestra—Dissipation—Ladies' Habits—The Bucentors—Beggars—Sweet Manners—Theatres—Priests—Coffee—Business and Pleasure—A Tame Pigeon—Lent—Government—The Brenta—Prejudice against Coal.

WE went down the Brenta in a barge that brought us in eight hours to Venice, the first appearance of which revived all the ideas inspired by Canaletti, whose views of this town are most scrupulously exact—those especially which one sees at the Queen of England's house in St. James's Park—to such a degree, indeed, that we knew all the famous towers, steeples, etc., before we reached them.

St. Mark's Place, after all I had read and all I had heard of it, exceeded expectation; such a cluster of excellence, such a constellation of artificial beauties, my mind had never ventured to excite the idea of within herself.

So great is the devotion of the common people here to their titular saint, that when they cry out, as we do, 'Old England for ever!' they do not say, 'Viva Venezia!' but 'Viva San Marco!' And I doubt much if that was not once the way with us. In one of Shakespeare's plays an expiring prince, being near to give all up for gone, is animated by his son in these words, 'Courage, father: cry "St. George!"'

We had an opportunity of seeing his day celebrated with a very grand procession the other morning, April 23rd, when a live boy personated the hero of the show, but sat so still upon his painted courser that it was long before I perceived him to breathe. The streets were vastly crowded with spectators, that in every place make the principal part of the spectacle.

It is odd that a custom which in contemplation seems so unlikely to please, should, when put in practice, appear highly necessary, and productive of an effect which can be obtained no other way. Were the houses in Parliament Street to hang damask curtains, worked carpets, pieces of various coloured silks with fringe or lace round them, out of every window when the King of England goes to the House, with numberless well-dressed ladies leaning out to see him pass, it would give one an idea of the continental towns upon a gala-day. But our people would be apt to cry out 'Monmouth Street!' and look ashamed if their neighbours saw the same deckerwork counterpane or crimson curtain produced at Easter which made a figure at Christmas the December before, so that no end would be put to expense in our country were such a fancy to take place. The rainy weather, beside, would spoil all our finery at once; and here, though it is still cold enough, to be sure, and the women wear satins, yet still one shivers over a bad fire only because there is no place to walk and warm one's self; for I have not seen a drop of rain. The truth is, this town cannot be a wholesome one, for there is scarcely a possibility of taking exercise; nor have I been once able to circulate my blood by motion since our arrival, except perhaps by climbing the beautiful tower which stands (as everything else does) in St. Mark's Place. And you may drive a garden-chair up that, so easy is the ascent, so broad and luminous the way. From the top is presented to one's sight the most striking of all prospects—water bounded by land, not land by water. The curious and elegant islets—upon which, and into which, the piles of Venice are driven, exhibiting clusters of houses, churches, palaces, everything—started up in the midst of the sea, so as to excite amazement.

VENICE: THE PIERA DEL BANDO.
From an Etching by Canaletto.

It was upon the day appointed for making a new chancellor, however, that one ought to have looked at this lovely city, when every shop, adorned with its own peculiar produce, was disposed to hail the passage of its favourite in a manner so lively, so luxuriant, and at the same time so tasteful—there's no telling. Milliners crowned the new dignitary's picture with flowers, while columns of gauze, twisted round with ribbon in the most elegant style, supported the figure on each side, and made the prettiest appearance possible. The furrier formed his skins into representations of the animal they had once belonged to; so the lion was seen dandling the kid at one door, while the fox stood courting a badger out of his hole at the other. The poulterers and fruiterers' were by many thought the most beautiful shops in town, from the variety of fancies displayed in the disposal of their goods; and I admired at the truly Italian ingenuity of a gunsmith, who had found the art of turning his instruments of terror into objects of delight by his judicious manner of placing and arranging them. Every shop was illuminated with a large glass chandelier before it, besides the wax candles and coloured lamps interspersed among the ornaments within. The senators have much the appearance of our lawyers going robed to Westminster Hall, but the gentiluomini, as they are called, wear red dresses, and remind me of the doctors of the ecclesiastical courts in Doctors' Commons.

I have said nothing yet about the gondolas, which everybody knows are black, and give an air of melancholy at first sight, yet are nothing less than sorrowful; it is like painting the lively Mrs. Cholmondeley in the character of Milton's

> ' Pensive nun, devout and pure,
> Sober, steadfast, and demure '—

as I once saw her drawn by a famous hand, to show a Venetian lady in her gondola and zendaletto, which is black like the gondola, but wholly calculated like that for the purposes of refined gallantry. So is the nightly rendezvous, the coffee-house and casino; for, whilst Palladio's palaces serve to adorn the grand canal and strike those who enter Venice with surprise at its magnificence, those snug retreats are intended for the relaxation of those who inhabit the more splendid apartments and are fatigued with exertions of dignity and necessity of no small expense.

We have been told much of the suspicious temper of Venetian laws, and have heard often that every discourse is suffered, except such as tends to political conversation, in this city; and that whatever nobleman, native of Venice, is seen speaking familiarly with a foreign minister runs a risk of punishment too terrible to be thought on.

How far that manner of proceeding may be wise or just, I know not; certain it is that they have preserved their laws inviolate, their city unattempted, and their republic respectable, through all the concussions that have shaken the rest of Europe. Surrounded by envious powers, it becomes them to be vigilant; conscious of the value of their unconquered State, it is no wonder that they love her; and surely the true *amor patriæ* never glowed more warmly in old Roman bosoms than in theirs, who draw, as many families here do, their pedigree from the consuls of the commonwealth. Love without jealousy is seldom to be met with, especially in these warm climates; let us, then, permit them to be jealous of a constitution which all the other States of Italy look on with envy not unmixed with malice, and propagate strange stories to its disadvantage.

That suspicion should be concealed under the mask of gaiety is neither very new nor very strange. The reign of our Charles II. was equally famous for plots, perjuries and cruel chastisements, as for wanton levity and indecent frolics. But here at

Venice there are no unpermitted frolics; her rulers love to see her gay and cheerful; they are the fathers of their country, and, if they indulge, take care not to spoil her.

With regard to common chat, I have heard many a liberal and eloquent disquisition upon the state of Europe in general, and on Venice in particular, from several agreeable friends at their own casino, who did not appear to have more fears upon them than myself, and I know not why they should. Chevalier Emo is deservedly a favourite with them, and we used to talk whole evenings of him and of General Elliott, the bombarding of Tunis and defence of Gibraltar. The newspapers spoke of some fireworks exhibited in England in honour of their hero; they were 'vraiment feux de joye,' said an agreeable Venetian; they were not 'feux d'artifice.'

Whoever sees St. Mark's Place lighted up of an evening, adorned with every excellence of human art and pregnant with pleasure, expressed by intelligent countenances sparkling with every grace of nature, the sea washing its walls, the moonbeams dancing on its subjugated waves, sport and laughter resounding from the coffee-houses, girls with guitars skipping about the square, masks and merry-makers singing as they pass you, unless a barge with a band of music is heard at some distance upon the water, and calls attention to sounds made sweeter by the element over which they are brought—whoever is led suddenly, I say, to this scene of seemingly perennial gaiety, will be apt to cry out of Venice, as Eve says to Adam in Milton :

> 'With thee conversing I forget all time,
> All seasons and their change—all please alike.'

For it is sure there are in this town many astonishing privations of all that are used to make other places delightful; and as poor Omai, the savage, said, when about to return to Otaheite : ' No horse there, no ass, no cow, no golden pippins, no dish of tea ! Ah, missey ! I go without everything—I always so content there though.'

It is really just so one lives at this lovely Venice. One has heard of a horse being exhibited for a show there, and yesterday I watched the poor people paying a penny a-piece for the sight of a stuffed one, and am more than persuaded of the truth of what I am told here—that numberless inhabitants live and die in this great capital, nor ever find out or think of inquiring how the milk brought from *terra firma* is originally produced.

The view of Venice from the Zueca—a word contracted from Giudecca, as I am told—would invite one never more to stray from it—farther, at least, than to St. George's Church, on another little opposite island, whence the prospect is surely wonderful. It was to this church I was sent for the purpose of seeing a famous picture, painted by Paul Veronese, of the marriage at Cana in Galilee. When we arrived, the picture was kept in a refectory belonging to friars (of what order I have forgotten), and no woman could be admitted. My disappointment was so great that I was deprived even of the powers of solicitation by the extreme ill-humour it occasioned, and my few entreaties for admission were completely disregarded by the good old monk, who remained outside with me, while the gentlemen visited the convent without molestation. At my return to Venice I met little comfort, as everybody told me it was my own fault, for I might put on men's clothes and see it whenever I pleased, as nobody then would stop, though perhaps all of them would know me.

But it is almost time to talk of the Rialto, said to be the finest single arch in Europe, and I suppose it is so—very beautiful, too, when looked on from the water, but so dirtily kept and deformed with mean shops, that, passing over it, disgust gets the better of every other sensation. The truth is, our dear

VENICE: THE ISLAND OF SAN GIORGIO.
After F. Guardi.

Venetians are nothing less than cleanly. St. Mark's Place is all covered over in a morning with chicken-coops, which stink one to death, as nobody, I believe, thinks of changing their baskets; and all about the ducal palace is made so very offensive by the resort of human creatures for every purpose most unworthy of so charming a place, that all enjoyment of its beauties is rendered difficult to a person of any delicacy, and poisoned so provokingly, that I do never cease to wonder that so little police and proper regulation are established in a city so particularly lovely to render her sweet and wholesome.

I have asked several friends about the truth of what one has been always hearing of in England—that the Venetian gondoliers sing Tasso's and Ariosto's verses in the streets at night, sometimes quarrelling with each other concerning the merits of their favourite poets; but what I have been told since I came here of their attachment to their respective masters, and secrecy when trusted by them in love affairs, seems far more probable, as they are proud to excess when they serve a nobleman of high birth, and will tell you with an air of importance that the house of Memmo, Monsenigo, or Gratterola has been served by their ancestors for these eighty or perhaps a hundred years, transmitting family pride thus from generation to generation, even when that pride is but reflected only like the mock rainbow of a summer sky. But hark! while I am writing this peevish reflection in my room, I hear some voices under my window answering each other upon the Grand Canal. It is—it *is* the gondolieri sure enough; they are at this moment singing to an odd sort of tune, but in no unmusical manner, the flight of Erminia from Tasso's 'Jerusalem.'

Apropos to singing, we were this evening carried to a well-known conservatory called the Mendicanti, who performed an oratorio in the church with great, and I dare say deserved, applause. It was difficult for me to persuade myself that all the performers were women, till, watching carefully, our eyes convinced us, as they were but slightly grated. The sight of girls, however, handling the double bass and blowing into the bassoon did not much please me; and the deep-toned voice of her who sung the part of Saul, seemed an odd, unnatural thing enough. What I found most curious and pretty was to hear Latin verses of the old leonine race broken into eight and six, and sung in rhyme by these women, as if they were airs of Metastasio—all in their dulcified pronunciation, too, for the patois runs equally through every language when spoken by a Venetian.

Well, these pretty sirens were delighted to seize upon us, and pressed our visit to their parlour with a sweetness that I know not who would have resisted. We had no such intent, and amply did their performance repay my curiosity for visiting Venetian beauties so justly celebrated for their seducing manners and soft address. They accompanied their voices with the forte-piano, and sung a thousand buffo songs with all that gay voluptuousness for which their country is renowned.

The state of music in Italy, if one may believe those who ought to know it best, is not what it was. The manner of singing is much changed, I am told, and some affectations have been suffered to encroach upon their natural graces. Among the persons who exhibited their talents at the Countess of Rosenberg's last week, our country-woman's performance was most applauded; but when I name Lady Clarges, no one will wonder.

It is said that painting is now but little cultivated among them Rome will, however, be the place for such inquiries. Angelica Kauffman being settled there seems a proof of their taste for living merit, and if one thing more than another evinces Italian candour and true good-nature, it is perhaps their generous willingness to be ever happy in acknowledging foreign excellence, and their delight in bringing forward the eminent qualities of every other nation, never insolently vaunting or bragging of their own. Unlike to this is the national spirit and confined ideas of perfection inherent in a Gallic mind, whose sole politeness is an *appliqué* stuck upon the coat, but never embroidered into it.

Among the noble senators of Venice, meantime, many good scholars, many belles lettres conversers, and, what is more valuable, many thinking men, may be found, and found hourly, who employ their powers wholly in care for the State, and make their pleasure, like true patriots, out of her felicity. The ladies, indeed, appear to study but one science:

> ' And where the lesson taught
> Is but to please, can pleasure seem a fault ?'

Like all sensualists, however, they fail of the end proposed, from hurry to obtain it, and consume those charms which alone can procure them continuance or change of admirers; they injure their health, too, irreparably, and that in their earliest youth, for few remain unmarried till fifteen, and at thirty have a wan and faded look. ' On ne goute pas ses plaisirs ici, on les avale,'* said Madame la Présidente yesterday very judiciously.

To try Venetian dames by English rules would be worse than all the tyranny complained of when some East Indian was condemned upon the Coventry Act for slitting his wife's nose—a common practice in his country, and perfectly agreeable to custom and the *usage du pays*. Here is no struggle for female education, as with us, no resources in study, no duties of family management; no bill of fare to be looked over in the morning, no accountbook to be settled at noon; no necessity of reading, to supply without disgrace the evening's chat; no laughing at the card-table, or twittering in the corner if a *lapsus linguæ* has produced a mistake, which malice never fails to record. A lady in Italy is sure of applause, so she takes little pains to obtain it. A Venetian lady has in particular so sweet a manner naturally, that she really charms without any settled intent to do so, merely from that irresistible good-humour and mellifluous tone of voice which seize the soul and detain it in despite of Juno-like majesty or Minerva-like wit. Nor ever was there prince or shepherd—Paris, I think, was both—who would not have bestowed his apple here.

* 'They do not taste their pleasures here; they swallow them whole.'

Meanwhile, my countryman, Howel, laments that the women at Venice are so little. But why so? The diminutive progeny of Vulcan, the Cabirs mysteriously adored of old, were of a size below that of the least living woman, if we believe Herodotus, and they were worshipped with more constant as well as more fervent devotion than the symmetrical goddess of beauty herself.

A custom which prevails here of wearing little or no rouge, and increasing the native paleness of their skins by scarce lightly wiping the very white powder from their faces, is a method no French woman of quality would like to adopt; yet surely the Venetians are not behindhand in the art of gaining admirers, and they do not, like their painters, depend upon colouring to ensure it.

Nothing can be a greater proof of the little consequence which dress gives to a woman than the reflection one must make on a Venetian lady's mode of appearance in her zendalet, without which nobody stirs out of their house in a morning. It consists of a full black silk petticoat, sloped just to train a very little on the ground, and flounced with gauze of the same colour. A skeleton wire upon the head, such as we use to make up hats, throwing loosely over it a large piece of black mode or persian, so as to shade the face like a curtain, the front being trimmed with a very deep black lace or souflet gauze, infinitely becoming. The thin silk that remains to be disposed of they roll back so as to discover the bosom, fasten it with a puff before at the top of their stomacher, and, once more rolling it back from the shape, tie it gracefully behind, and let it hang in two long ends.

The evening ornament is a silk hat, shaped like a man's, and of the same colour, with a white or worked lining at most, and sometimes one feather; a great black silk cloak, lined with white, and perhaps a narrow border down before, with a vast, heavy round handkerchief of black lace, which lies over neck and shoulders, and conceals shape and all completely. Here is surely little appearance of art, no craping or frizzing the hair, which is flat at the top and all of one length, hanging in long curls about the back or sides as it happens. No brown powder, and no rouge at all. Thus without variety does a Venetian lady contrive to delight the eye, and without much instruction, too, to charm the ear. A source of thought fairly cut off beside, in giving her no room to show taste in dress or invent new fancies and disposition of ornaments for to-morrow. The Government takes all that trouble off her hands, knows every pin she wears, and where to find her at any moment of the day or night.

Meantime, nothing conveys to a British observer a stronger notion of loose living and licentious dissoluteness than the sight of one's servants, gondoliers, and other attendants on the scenes and circles of pleasure, where you find them, though never drunk, dead with sleep upon the stairs, or in their boats, or in the open street for that matter, like over-swilled voters at an election in England. One may trample on them if one will, they hardly can be awakened; and their companions, who have more life left, set the others literally on their feet to make them capable of obeying their master or lady's call. With all this appearance of levity, however, there is an unremitted attention to the affairs of state, nor is any senator seen to come late or negligently to council next day, however he may have amused himself all night.

The sight of the Bucentoro prepared for gala, and the glories of Venice upon Ascension Day, must now put an end to other observations. We had the honour and comfort of seeing all from a galley belonging to a noble Venetian Bragadin, whose civilities to us were singularly kind as well as extremely polite. His attentions did not cease with the morning show, which we shared in common with numbers of fashionable people that filled his ship and partook of his profuse, elegant refreshments, but he followed us after dinner to the house of our English friends, and took six of us together in a gay bark, adorned with his arms and rowed by eight gondoliers in superb liveries made up for the occasion to match the boat, which was like them white, blue and silver, a flag of the same colours flying from the stern—till we arrived at the Corso—so they call the place of contention where the rowers exert their skill and ingenuity; and numberless oars dashing the waves at once make the only agitation of which the sea seems capable; while ladies, now no longer dressed in black, but ornamented with all their jewels, flowers, etc., display their beauties unveiled upon the water, and, covering the lagoons with gaiety and splendour, bring to one's mind the games in Virgil and the galley of Cleopatra by turns.

The Bucentoro holds two hundred people, and is heavy besides with statues, columns, etc., the top covered with crimson velvet, and the sides enlivened by twenty-one oars on each hand. Musical performers attend in another barge, while foreigners in gilded pajots increase the general show. Meantime, the vessel that contains the doge, etc., carries him slowly out to sea, where, in presence of his senators, he drops a plain gold ring into the water, with these words, 'Desponsamus te mare, in signum veri perpetuique dominii.'*

Our weather was favourable, and the people all seemed happy. When the ceremony is put off from day to day, it naturally damps their spirits, and produces superstitious presages of an unlucky year; nor is that strange, for the season of storms ought surely to be passed in a climate so celebrated for mildness and equanimity. The praises of Italian weather, though wearisomely frequent among us, seem, however, much confined to this island, for aught I see, who am often tired with hearing their complaints of their own sky now that they are under it—always too cold or too hot, or a sciroc wind, or a rainy day, or a hard frost, 'che gela fin ai pensieri,'† or something to murmur about, while their only great nuisances pass unnoticed—the heaps of dirt and crowds of beggars, who infest the streets and poison the pleasures of society. While ladies are eating ice at a coffee-house door, while decent people are hearing mass at the altar, while strangers are surveying the beauties of the place—no peace, no enjoyment can one obtain for the beggars, numerous beyond credibility, saucy and airy and odd in their manners, and exhibiting such various lamenesses

---

* 'We espouse thee, O sea! in sign of true and perpetual dominion.'
† Which freezes even one's fancy.

and horrible deformities in their figure, that I can sometimes hardly believe my eyes, but am willing to be told, what is not very improbable, that many of them come from a great distance to pass the season of Ascension here at Venice. I never, indeed, saw anything so gently endured which it appeared so little difficult to remedy; but though, I hope, it would be hard to find a place where more alms are asked or less are given than in Venice, yet I never saw refusals so pleasantly softened as by the manners of the high Italians towards the low. Ladies in particular are so soft-mouthed, so tender in replying to those who have their lot cast far below them, that one feels one's own harsher disposition corrected by their sweetness; and when they called my maid sister, in good time, pressing her hand with affectionate kindness, it melted me; though I feared from time to time there must be hypocrisy at bottom of such sugared words, till I caught a lady of condition yesterday turning to the window and praying fervently for the girl's conversion to Christianity, all from a tender and pious emotion of her gentle heart: as, notwithstanding their caresses, no man is more firmly persuaded of a mathematical truth than they are of mine and my maid's living in a state of certain and eternal reprobation — 'Ma fanno veramente vergogna a noi altri,'* say they, quite in the spirit of the old Romans, who thought all nations barbarous except their own.

A woman of quality, near whom I sat at the fine ball Bragadin made two nights ago in honour of this gay season, inquired how I had passed the morning. I named several churches I had looked into, particularly that which they esteem beyond the rest as a favourite work of Palladio, and called the Redentore.

'You do very right,' says she, 'to look at our churches, as you have none in England, I know; but then you have so many other fine things—such charming steel buttons, for example,' pressing my hand to show that she meant no offence; 'for,' added she, 'chi pensa d'una maniera, chi pensa d'un' altra.'†

Here are many theatres, the worst infinitely superior to ours, the best as far below those of Milan and Turin; but, then, here are other diversions, and everyone's dependence for pleasure is not placed upon the opera. They have now thrown up a sort of temporary wall of painted canvas, in an oval form, within St. Mark's Place, profusely illuminated round the new-formed walk, which is covered in at

* 'But they really shame even us.'
† 'One person is of one mind, you know, another of another.'

top, and adorned with shops round the right-hand side, with pillars to support the canopy, the lamps, etc., on the left hand. This open Ranelagh, so suited to the climate, is exceedingly pleasing. Here is room to sit, to chat, to saunter up and down, from two o'clock in the morning, when the opera ends, till a hot sun sends us all home to rest—for late hours must be complied with at Venice, or you can have no diversion at all, as the earliest casino belonging to your soberest friends has not a candle lighted in it till past midnight.

It strikes a person who has lived some months in other parts of Italy to see so very few clergymen at Venice, and none hardly who have much the look or air of a man of fashion. Milan, though such heavy complaints are daily made there of encroachments on Church power and depredations on Church opulence, still swarms with ecclesiastics, and in an assembly of thirty people there are never fewer than ten or twelve at the very least. But here it should seem as if the political cry of 'Fuori i preti!'* which is said loudly in the council-chamber before any vote is suffered to pass into a law, were carried in the conversation rooms, too, for a priest is here less frequent than a clergyman at London, and those

* 'Out with the clergy !'

one sees about are almost all ordinary men, decent and humble in their appearance, of a bashful, distant carriage, like the parson of the parish in North Wales, or *le curé du village* in the south of France, and seem no way related to an Abate of Milan or Turin, still less to Monsieur l'Abbé at Paris.

Though this Republic has long maintained a sort of independency from the court of Rome, having shown themselves weary of the Jesuits two hundred years before any other potentate dismissed them, while many of the Venetian populace followed them about, crying, 'Andate, andate, niente pigliate, e mai ritornate!'*—and although there is a patriarch here who takes care of Church matters, and is attentive to keep his clergy from ever meddling with or even mentioning affairs of state, as in such a case the Republic would not scruple punishing them as laymen—yet has Venice kept, as they call it, St. Peter's boat from sinking more than once, when she saw the Pope's territories endangered or his sovereignty insulted; nor is there any city more eminent for the decency with which Divine service is administered, or for the devout and decorous behaviour of individuals at the time any sacred office is performing. She has ever behaved like a true Christian potentate, keeping her faith firm and her honour

---

* 'Begone, begone; nothing take, nor turn anon.'

scrupulously clear in all treaties and conventions with other States, fewer instances being given of Venetian falsehood or treachery towards neighbouring nations than of any other European power, excepting only Britain, her truly beloved ally, with whom she never had a difference, and whose cause was so warmly espoused last war by the inhabitants of this friendly State, that numbers of young nobility were willing to run a-volunteering in her defence, but that the laws of Venice forbid her nobles ranging from home without leave given from the State. It was, therefore, not an ill saying, though an old one perhaps, that the government of Venice was rich and consolatory like its treacle, being compounded nicely of all the other forms—a grain of monarchy, a scruple of democracy, a drachm of oligarchy, and an ounce of aristocracy—as the *teriaca* so much esteemed is said to be a composition of the four principal drugs, but can never be got genuine except here, at the original dispensary.

Indeed, the longevity of this incomparable commonwealth is a certain proof of its temperance, exercise, and cheerfulness, the great preservatives in every body, politic as well as natural. Nor should the love of peace be left out of her eulogium, who has so often reconciled contending princes, that Thuanus gave her, some centuries ago, due praise for her pacific disposition, so necessary to the health of a commercial State, and called her city 'civilis prudentiæ officina.'

Another reason may be found for the long-continued prosperity of Venice in her constant adherence to a precept, the neglect of which must at length shake, or, rather, loosen the foundations of every State; for it is a maxim here, handed down from generation to generation, that change breeds more mischief from its novelty than advantage from its utility.

The patriotism inherent in the breasts of individuals makes another strong cause of this State's exemption from decay; they say themselves that the soul of old Rome has transmigrated to Venice, and that every galley which goes into action considers itself as charged with the fate of the commonwealth. 'Dulce et decorum est pro patria mori' seems a sentence grown obsolete in other Italian States, but is still in full force here; and I doubt not but the high-born and high-souled ladies of this day would willingly, as did their generous ancestors in 1600, part with their rings, bracelets, every ornament, to make ropes for those ships which defend their dearer country.

The perpetual state of warfare maintained by this

nation against the Turks has never lessened nor cooled. Their vicinity to Turkey has, however, made them contract some similarity of manners; for what, except being imbued with Turkish notions, can account for the people's rage here, young and old, rich and poor, to pour down such quantities of coffee? I have already had seven cups to-day, and feel frightened lest we should some of us be killed with so strange an abuse of it. On the opposite shore, across the Adriatic, opium is taken to counteract its effects; but these dear Venetians have no notion of sleep being necessary to their existence, I believe, as some or other of them seem constantly in motion, and there is really no hour of the four-and-twenty in which the town seems perfectly still and quiet.

I am persuaded if one were to live here (which could not be for long, I think), he should forget the use of sleep; for what with the market folks bringing up the boats from *terra firma* loaded with every produce of nature, neatly arranged in these flat-bottomed conveyances, the coming up of which begins about three o'clock in a morning and ends about six; the gondoliers rowing home their masters and ladies about that hour, and so on till eight; the common business of the town, which it is then time to begin; the state affairs and *pregai*, which often, like our House of Commons, sit late, and detain many gentlemen from the circles of morning amusements—that I find very entertaining, particularly the street orators and mountebanks in Piazza St. Marco; the shops and stalls where chickens, ducks, etc., are sold by auction, comically enough, to the highest bidder, a flourishing fellow, with a hammer in his hand, shining away in character of auctioneer; the crowds which fill the courts of judicature when any cause of consequence is to be tried; the clamorous voices, keen observations, poignant sarcasms, and acute contentions carried on by the advocates, who seem more awake, or, in their own phrase, *svelti*, than all the rest: all these things take up so much time, that twenty-four hours do not suffice for the business and diversions of Venice, where dinner must be eaten as in other places, though I can scarcely find a minute to spare for it, while such fish waits one's knife and fork as I most certainly did never see before, and as I suppose are not to be seen in any sea but this in such perfection. Fresh sturgeon (*ton*, as they call it), and fresh anchovies, large as herrings, and dressed like sprats in London, incomparable; turbots, like those of Torbay exactly, and plentiful as there, with enormous pipers, are what one principally eats here,

VENICE BY NIGHT.

From an Engraving after G. B. Moretti.

The fried liver, without which an Italian can hardly go on from day to day, is so charmingly dressed at Milan, that I grew to like it as well as they; but at Venice it is sad stuff, and they call it *fegao*.

Well, the ladies, who never hardly dine at all, rise about seven in the evening, when the gentlemen are just got ready to attend them, and sit sipping their chocolate on a chair at the coffee-house door with great tranquillity, chatting over the common topics of the times; nor do they appear half so shy of each other as the Milanese ladies, who seldom seem to have any pleasure in the soft converse of a female friend. But though certainly no women can be more charming than these Venetian dames, they have forgotten the old mythological fable that the youngest of the Graces was married to sleep.

There are men here, however, who, because they are not quite in the gay world, keep themselves awake whole nights at study; and much has been told me of a collection of books belonging to a private scholar, Pinelli, who goes very little out, as worthy attentive examination.

All literary topics are pleasingly discussed at Quirini's Casino, where everything may be learned by the conversation of the company, as Doctor Johnson said of his literary club, but more agreeably, because women are always half the number of persons admitted here.

One evening our society was amused by the entrance of a foreign nobleman, exactly what we should in London emphatically call a character—learned, loud and overbearing, though of a carriage that impressed great esteem. I have not often listened to so well-furnished a talker, nor one more capable of giving great information. He had seen the Pyramids of Egypt, he told us, had climbed Mount Horeb, and visited Damascus; but possessed the art of detaining our attention more on himself than on the things or places he harangued about; for conversation that can scarcely be called, where one man holds the company suspended on his account of matters pompously, though instructively, related. He stayed here a very little while among us—is a native of France, a grandee of Spain, a man of uncommon talents, and a traveller. I should be sorry never to meet him more.

An odd thing, to which I was this morning witness, has called my thoughts away to a curious train of reflections upon the animal race, and how far they may be made companionable and intelligent. The famous Ferdinand Bertoni, so well-known in London by his long residence among us, and from the undisputed merit of his compositions, now inhabits this his native city, and, being fond of dumb creatures, as we call them, took to petting a pigeon, one of the few animals which can live at Venice, where, as I observed, scarcely any quadrupeds can be admitted, or would exist with any degree of comfort to themselves. This creature has, however, by keeping his master company, I trust, obtained so perfect an ear and taste for music, that no one who sees his behaviour can doubt for a moment of the pleasure he takes in hearing Mr. Bertoni play and sing; for as soon as he sits down to the instrument, Columbo begins shaking his wings, perches on the pianoforte, and expresses the most indubitable emotions of delight. If, however, he or anyone else strike a note false, or make any kind of discord upon the keys, the dove never fails to show evident tokens of anger and distress, and, if teased too long, grows quite enraged, pecking the offender's legs and fingers in such a manner as to leave nothing less doubtful than the sincerity of his resentment. Signora Cecilia Giuliani, a scholar of Bertoni's, who has received some overtures from the London theatre lately, will, if she ever arrives there, bear testimony to the truth of an assertion very difficult to believe, and to which I should hardly myself give credit, were I not witness to it every morning that I choose to call and confirm my own belief. A friend present protested he should feel afraid to touch the harpsichord before so nice a critic, and, though we all laughed at the assertion, Bertoni declared he never knew the bird's judgment fail, and that he often kept him out of the room for fear of his affronting or tormenting those who came to take musical instructions. With regard to other actions of life, I saw nothing particular in the pigeon but his tameness and strong attachment to his master; for, though never winged, and only clipped a very little, he never seeks to range away from the house or quit his master's service.

I do think the Turkish sailor gave an admirable account of a carnival when he told his Mahometan friends at his return that those poor Christians were all disordered in their senses and nearly in a state of actual madness, while he remained among them, till one day, on a sudden, they luckily found out a certain gray powder that cured such symptoms, and, laying it on their heads one Wednesday morning, the wits of all the inhabitants were happily restored at a stroke; the people grew sober, quiet and composed, and went about their business just like other folks. He meant the ashes strewed on the heads of all one meets in the streets through many a Catholic country, when all masquerading, money-making, etc., subside

CARNIVAL SCENE.
After Tiepolo.

for forty days, and give, from the force of the contrast, a greater appearance of devotion and decorous behaviour in Venice than almost anywhere else during Lent.

The Venetians, to confess the truth, are not quite so strenuously bent on the unattainable felicity of finding every man in the same mind as others of the Italians are, and one great reason why they are more gay and less malignant, have fewer strong prejudices than others of their countrymen, is merely because they are happier. Most of the second rank, and, I believe, all of the first rank among them, have some share in governing the rest; it is therefore necessary to exclude ignorance, and natural to encourage social pleasures. Each individual feels his own importance, and scorns to contribute to the degradation of the whole by indulging a gross depravity of manners, or at least of principles. Every person lifted one degree from the lowest finds it his interest as well as duty to love his country, and lend his little support to the general fabric of a state they all know how to respect, while the very vulgar willingly perform the condition exacted and punctually pay obedience for protection. They have an unlimited confidence in their rulers, who live amongst them, and can desire only their utmost good. How they are governed comes seldom into their heads to inquire. 'Che ne pensa lù,'* says a low Venetian, if you ask him, and humorously points at a Clarissimo passing by while you talk. They have, indeed, all the reason to be certain that where the power is divided among such numbers, one will be sure to counteract another if mischief towards the whole be intended.

The subjects of this republic resident in the capital are less savage and more happy than those who live upon the *terra firma*, where many outrages are still committed, disgraceful to the State, from the mere facility offenders find either in escaping to the dominion of other princes, or of finding shelter at home from the madly-bestowed protection these old barons on the Continent cease not yet to give to ruffians who profess their service and acknowledge dependence upon them. In the town, however, little is known of these enormities, and less is talked on; and what information has come to my ears of the murders done at Brescia and Bergamo was given me at Milan, where Blainville's accounts of that country, though written so long ago, did not fail to receive confirmation from the lips of those who knew perfectly well what they were talking about. And I am told that Labbia—Giovanni Labbia, the new Podestà

* 'Let him look to that.'

sent to Brescia—has worked wonderful reformation among the inhabitants of that territory, where I am ashamed to relate the computation of subjects lost to the State by being killed in cold blood during the years 1780 and 1781.

I see that I have said more about Venice, where I have lived five weeks, than about Milan, where I stayed five months.

On Saturday next I am to forsake—but I hope not for ever—this gay, this gallant city, so often described, so certainly admired—seen with rapture, quitted with regret. Seat of enchantment! headquarters of pleasure, farewell!

> ' Leave us as we ought to be,
> Leave the Britons rough and free.'

It was on the 21st of May, then, that we returned up the Brenta in a barge to Padua, stopping from time to time to give refreshment to our conductors and their horse, which draws on the side, as one sees them at Richmond, where the banks are scarcely more beautifully adorned by art than here by nature, though the Brenta is a much narrower river than the Thames at Richmond, and its villas, so justly celebrated, far less frequent. The sublimity of their architecture, however, the magnificence of their orangeries, the happy construction of the cool arcades, and general air of festivity which breathes upon the banks of this truly wizard stream, planted with dancing, not weeping, willows, to which on a bright evening the lads and lasses run for shelter from the sunbeams—

<blockquote>' Et fugit ad salices, et se cupit ante videri,'*</blockquote>

are, I suppose, peculiar to itself, and best described by Monsieur de Voltaire, whose Pococurante, the Venetian senator in 'Candide,' that possesses all delights in his villa upon the banks of the Brenta, is a very lively portrait, and would be natural, too, but that Voltaire, as a Frenchman, could not forbear making his character speak in a very un-Italian manner, boasting of his felicity in a style they never use; for they are really no puffers, no vaunters of that which they possess—make no disgraceful comparisons between their own rarities and the want of them in other countries, nor offend you, as the French do, with false pity and hateful consolations.

If anything in England seem to excite their wonder and ill-placed compassion, it is our coal-fires, which they persist in thinking strangely unwholesome, and a melancholy proof that we are grievously devoid of wood before we can prevail upon

---

* ' While tripping to the wood my wanton hies,
  She wishes to be seen before she flies.'

A Barge on the Brenta.

ourselves to dig the bowels of old earth for fuel, at the hazard of our precious health, if not of its certain loss; nor could I convince the wisest man I tried at, that wood burnt to chark is a real poison, while it would be difficult by any process of chemistry to force much evil out of coal. They are steadily of opinion that consumptions are occasioned by these fires, and that all the subjects of Great Britain are consumptively disposed, merely because those who are so go into Italy for change of air, though I never heard that the wood-smoke helped their breath, or a brazier full of ashes under the table their appetite. Meantime, whoever seeks to convince instead of persuade an Italian, will find he has been employed in a Sisyphean labour; the stone may roll to the top, but is sure to return and rest at his feet who had courage to try the experiment. Logic is a science they love not, and, I think, steadily refuse to cultivate; nor is argument a style of conversation they naturally affect—as Lady Macbeth says, 'Question enrageth him'—and the dialogues of Socrates would to them be as disgusting as the violence of Xantippe.

Now, then, I must leave this lovely state of Venice, where, if the paupers in every town of it did not crowd about one, tormenting passengers with unextinguishable clamour, and surrounding them with sights of horror unfit to be surveyed by any eyes except those of the surgeon, who should alleviate their anguish, or at least conceal their truly unspeakable distresses—one should break one's heart almost at the thoughts of quitting people who show such tenderness towards their friends, that less than ocular conviction would scarce persuade me to believe such wandering misery could remain disregarded among the most amiable and pleasing people in the world. His Excellency Bragadin half promised me that some steps should be taken at Venice at least to remove a nuisance so disgraceful, and said that when I came again I should walk about the town in white satin slippers, and never see a beggar from one end of it to the other.

CHAPTER V

FERRARA AND BOLOGNA

Small Population of Ferrara—An Improvisatore—Bologna—Religiousness of the People—Custom-house Officers—The King of Naples.

Ferrara, May, 1785.

THE road from Padua hither is not a good one, but so adorned one cares not much whether it is good or no—so sweetly are the mulberry-trees planted on each side, with vines richly festooning up and down them, as if for the decoration of a dance at the opera. One really expects the flower-girls with baskets or garlands, and scarcely can persuade one's self that all is real.

Never, sure, was anything more rejoicing to the heart than this lovely season in this lovely country. The city of Ferrara, too, is a fine one—Ferrara *la civile* the Italians call it, but it seems rather to merit the epithet *solenne,* so stately are its buildings, so wide and uniform its streets. My pen was just upon the point of praising its cleanliness, too, till I reflected there was nobody to dirty it. I looked half an hour before I could find one beggar—a bad account of poor Ferrara; but it brought to my mind how unreasonably my daughter and myself had laughed, seven years ago, at reading in an extract from some of the foreign gazettes how the famous improvisatore, Talassi, who was in England about the year 1770, and entertained with his justly-admired talents the literati at London, had published an account of his visit to Mr. Thrale, at a villa eight miles from Westminster Bridge, during that time, when he had the good fortune, he said, to meet many celebrated characters at his country-seat, and the mortification, which nearly overbalanced it, to miss seeing the immortal Garrick, then confined by illness. In all this, however, there was nothing ridiculous; but we fancied his description of Streatham village truly so when we read that he called it 'Luogo assai popolato ed ameno,'* an expression apparently pompous and inadequate to the subject. But the jest disappeared when I got into his town, a place which perhaps may be said to possess every other excellence but that of being 'popolato ed ameno;' and I sincerely believe that no Ferrara man could have missed making the same or a like observation, as in this finely-constructed city the grass literally grows in the street,

* 'A populous and delightful place.'

nor do I hear that the state of the air and water is such as is likely to tempt new inhabitants. How much, then, and how reasonably must he have wondered, and how easily must he have been led to express his wonder, at seeing a village no bigger than that of Streatham contain a number of people equal, as I doubt not but it does, to all the dwellers in Ferrara!

Mr. Talassi is reckoned in his own country a man of great genius; in ours he was, as I recollect, received with much attention as a person able and willing to give us demonstration that improviso verses might be made and sung extemporaneously to some well-known tune, generally one which admits of and requires very long lines, that so alternate rhymes may not be improper, as they give more time to think forward and gain a moment for composition. Of this power many, till they saw it done, did not believe the existence, and many, after they had seen it done, persisted in saying, perhaps in thinking, that it could be done only in Italian. I cannot, however, believe that they possess any exclusive privileges or supernatural gifts, though it will be hard to find one who thinks better of them than I do; but Spaniards can sing sequedillas under their mistresses' window well enough, and our Welsh people can make the harper sit down in the churchyard after service is over, and, placing themselves round him, command the instrument to go over some old song-tune, when, having listened awhile, one of the company forms a stanza of verses, which run to it in well-adapted measure, and as he ends another begins, continuing the tale or retorting the satire, according to the style in which the first began it—all this, too, in a language less perhaps than any other melodious to the ear, though Howel found out a resemblance between their prosody and that of the Italian writers in early days, when they held agnominations, or the enforcement of consonant words and syllables one upon the other, to be elegant in a more eminent degree than they do now. For example, in Welsh, ' Tewgris, todyrris, ty'r derrin, gwillt,' etc.; in Italian, ' Donne, O danno che felo affronto affronta ; in selva salvo a me,' with a thousand more. The whole secret of improvisation, however, seems to consist in this, that extempore verses are never written down, and one may easily conceive that much may go off well with a good voice in singing which no one would read if they were once registered by the pen.

I have already asserted that the Italians are not a laughing nation; were ridicule to step in among them, many innocent pleasures would soon be lost, and this among the first. For who would risk the making impromptu poems at Paris? *pour s'attirer persiflage* in every *coterie comme il faut?** or in London, at the hazard of being taken off and held up for a laughing-stock at every printseller's window? A man must have good courage in England before he ventures at diverting a little company by such devices, while one would yawn, and one would whisper, a third would walk gravely out of the room and say to his friend upon the stairs, ' Why, sure, we had better read our old poets at home, than be called together, like fools, to hear what comes uppermost in such-a-one's head about his Daphne! In good time! Why, I have been tired of Daphne since I was fourteen years old.' But the best jest of all would be to see an ordinary fellow—a strolling player, for example—set seriously to make or repeat verses in our streets or squares concerning his sweetheart's cruelty, when he would be in more danger from that of the mob and the magistrates, who, if the first did not throw dirt at him and drive him home quickly, would come themselves and examine into his sanity, and, if they found him not statutably mad, commit him for a vagrant.

Bologna.

This fat Bologna has a tristful look, from the numberless priests, friars, and women all dressed in

---

* To draw upon one's self the ridicule of every polite assembly.

black, who fill the streets, and stop on a sudden to pray when I see nothing done to call forth immediate addresses to Heaven. Extremes do certainly meet, however, and my Lord Peter in this place is so like his fanatical brother Jack, that I know not what is come to him. To-morrow is the day of Corpus Domini. Why it should be preceded by such dismal ceremonies, I know not; there is nothing melancholy in the idea, but we shall be sure of a magnificent procession.

So it was, too, and wonderfully well attended—noblemen and ladies, with tapers in their hands, and their trains borne by well-dressed pages, had a fine effect. All still in black:

> 'Black, but such as in esteem
> Prince Memnon's sister might beseem;
> With sable stole of cypress lawn,
> O'er their decent shoulders drawn.'

I never saw a spectacle so stately, so solemn a show, in my life before, and was much less tired of the long-continued march than were my Roman Catholic companions.

Our inn is not a good one; the Pellegrino is engaged for the King of Naples and his train. The place we are housed in is full of bugs and every odious vermin—no wonder, surely, where such oven-like porticoes catch and retain the heat as if constructed on set purpose so to do. The Montagnuola at night was something of relief, but contrary to every other resort of company, the less it is frequented the gayer it appears; for Nature there has been lavish of her bounties, which seem disregarded by the Bolognese, who unluckily find out that there is a burying-ground within view, though at no small distance really, and, planting themselves over against that, they stand or kneel for many minutes together in whole rows, praying, as I understand, for the souls which once animated the bodies of the people whom they believe to lie interred there—all this, too, even at the hours dedicated to amusement.

Cardinal Buon Compagni, the legate sent from Rome here, is gone home, and the vice-legate officiated in his place, much to the consolation of the inhabitants, who observed with little delight or gratitude his endeavours to improve their trade, or his care to maintain their privileges; while his natural disinclination to hypocritical manners, or what we so emphatically call cant, gave them an aversion to his person and dislike of his government, which he might have prevented by formality of look and very trifling compliances. But everything helps to prove that if you would please people, it must be done their way, not your own.

Here are some charming manufactures in this

town, and I fear it requires much self-denial in an English woman not to long at least for the fine crapes, tiffanies, etc., which might here be bought I know not how cheap, and would make one so happy in London or at Bath. But these Custom-house officers, these *rats de cave,* as the French comically call them, will not let a ribbon pass. Such is the restless jealousy of little States, and such their unremitted attention to keep the goods made in one place out of the gates of another. Few things upon a journey contribute to torment and disgust one more than the teasing inquiries at the door of every city—who one is, what one's name is, what one's rank in life or employment is—that so all may be written down and carried to the chief magistrate for his information, who immediately despatches a proper person to examine whether you gave in a true report—where you lodge, why you came, how long you mean to stay, with twenty more inquisitive speeches, which to a subject of more liberal Governments must necessarily appear impertinent as frivolous, and make all my hopes of bringing home the most trifling presents for a friend abortive. So there is an end of that felicity, and we must sit, like the girl at the fair described by Gay:

> ' Where the coy nymph knives, combs, and scissors spies,
> And looks on thimbles with desiring eyes.'

A church, situated on the only hill one can observe for miles, is dedicated to the Madonna St. Luc, as it is called. Before the figure of the Madonna I did see some men kneel with a truly idolatrous devotion. That it was painted by St. Luke is believed by them all.

The girls, who sit in clusters at the chapel-doors as one goes up, singing hymns in praise of the Virgin Mary, pleased me much, as it was a mode of veneration inoffensive to religion and agreeable to the fancy; but seeing them bow down to that black figure, in open defiance of the Decalogue, shocked me. Why all the very, very early pictures of the Virgin, and many of our blessed Saviour himself, done in the first ages of Christianity, should be black, or at least tawny, is to me wholly incomprehensible, nor could I ever yet obtain an explanation of its cause from men of learning or from connoisseurs.

Whilst I perambulated the palaces of the Bolognese nobility, gloomy though spacious, and melancholy though splendid, I could not but admire at Richardson's judgment when he makes his beautiful Bigot, his interesting Clementina, an inhabitant of superstitious Bologna. The unconquerable attachment she shows to original prejudices, and the horror of what she has been taught to consider as heresy, could scarcely have been attributed so happily to the dweller in any town but this, where I hear nothing but the sound of people saying their rosaries, and see nothing in the street but people telling their beads.

But the King of Naples is arrived, and that attention which wits and scholars can retain for centuries may not be unjustly paid to princes while they last.

Our Bolognese have hit upon an odd method of entertaining him, however—no other than making a representation of Mount Vesuvius on the Montagnuola, or place of evening resort, hoping at least to treat him with something new, I trow. Were the King of England to visit these *cari Bolognese*, surely they would show him Westminster Bridge, with a view of the Archbishop's palace at Lambeth on one side the river, and Somerset House on the other!

A pretty throne, or state box, was soon got in order, that it was, and the motion excited by carrying the fireworks to have them prepared for the evening's show gave life to the morning, which hung less heavily than usual ; nor did the people recollect the churchyard at a distance while the merry King of Naples was near them. His Majesty appeared perfectly contented and good-humoured, and happy with whatever was done for his amusement. I remember his behaviour at Milan, though, too well to be surprised at his pleasantness of disposition, when my maid' was delighted to see him dance among the girls at a Festa di Ballo, from whence I retired early myself and sent her back to enjoy it all in my domino. He played at cards too when at Milan, I recollect, in the common Ridotto Chamber at the theatre, and played for common sums, so as to charm everyone with his kindness and affability.

I am glad, however, that we shall now be soon released from this, upon the whole, disagreeable town, where there is the best possible food, too, for body and mind, but where the inhabitants seem to think only of the next world, and do little to amuse those who have not yet quite done with this. If they are sincere, meantime, God will bless them with a long continuance of the appellation they so justly deserve; and those travellers who pass through will find some amends in the rich cream and incomparable dinners every day for the insects that devour them every night, and will, if they are wise, seek compensation from the company of the half-animated pictures that crowd the palaces and churches for the half-dead inhabitants who kneel in the streets of Bologna.

CHAPTER VI

FLORENCE

Florence—An English Inn—Fruits and Flowers—St. John the Baptist's Day—A Cardinal—Horse Races—Chariot Races—Pantomimes—Unaffected Manners—Street Cries—The Grand Duke—Peasant Costumes—The Young Pretender—Dialects—Corilla—A Baby Friar—Speedy Burial.

WE slept nowhere, except perhaps in the carriage, between our last residence at Bologna and this delightful city, to which we passed apparently through a new region of the earth, or even air, clambering up mountains covered with snow, and viewing with amazement the little valleys between, where, after quitting the summer season, all glowing with heat and spread into verdure, we found cherry-trees in blossom, oaks and walnuts scarcely beginning to bud. These mountains are, however, much below those of Savoy for dignity and beauty of appearance, though high enough to be troublesome and barren enough to be desolate.

We arrived late at our inn—an English one they say it is—and many of the last miles were passed very pleasantly by my maid and myself in anticipating the comforts we should receive by finding ourselves among our own country folks. In good time! and by once more eating, sleeping, etc., all in the English way, as her phrase is. Accordingly, here are small, low beds again, soft and clean, and down pillows; here are currant tarts, which the Italians scorn to touch, but which we are happy and delighted to pay not ten, but twenty times their value for, because a currant tart is so much in the English way; and here are beans and bacon in a climate where it is impossible that bacon should be either wholesome or agreeable; and one eats infinitely worse than one did at Milan, Venice, or Bologna, and infinitely dearer, too; but that makes it still more completely in the English way.

The fruits in this place begin to astonish me; such cherries did I never yet see, or even hear tell of, as when I caught the laquais de place weighing two of them in a scale to see if they came to an ounce. These are, in the London street phrase, cherries like plums, in size at least, but in flavour they far exceed them, being exactly of the kind that we call bleeding-hearts, hard to the bite and parting easily from the stone, which is proportionately small. Figs, too, are here in such perfection, that it is not easy for an English gardener to guess at their excellence; for it is not by superior size, but taste and colour, that they are distinguished—small and green on the outside, a bright full crimson within—and we eat them with raw ham, and truly delicious is the dainty. By raw ham, I mean ham cured, not boiled or roasted. It is no wonder, though, that fruits should mature in such a sun as this is, which, to give a just notion of its penetrating fire, I will take leave to tell my country-women is so violent, that I use no other method of heating the pinching-irons to curl my hair than that of poking them out at a south window, with the handles shut in, and the glasses darkened to keep us from being actually fired in his beams. Before I leave off speaking about the fruit, I must add that both fig and cherry are produced by standards, that the strawberries here are small and high-flavoured, like our 'woods,' and that there are no other. England affords greater variety in that kind of fruit than any nation; and as to peaches, nectarines, or greengage plums, I have seen none yet. Lady Cowper has made us a present of a small pineapple, but the Italians have no taste to it. Here is sun enough to ripen them without hot-houses, I am sure, though they repeatedly told us at Milan and Venice that this was the coolest place to pass the summer in, because of the Apennine mountains shading us from the heat, which they confessed to be intolerable with them.

Here, however, they inform us that it is madness to retire into the country, as English people do, during the hot season; for, as there is no shade from high timber-trees, one is bit to death by animals—gnats in particular—which here are excessively troublesome even in the town, notwithstanding we scatter vinegar and use all the arts in our power; but the ground-floor is coolest, and everybody struggles to get themselves a *terreno*, as they call it.

Florence is full just now, and Mr. Jean Figliazzi, an intelligent gentleman who lives here and is well acquainted with both nations, says that all the genteel people come to take refuge *from* the country to Florence in July and August, as the subjects of Great Britain run *to* the country from the heats of London or Bath.

The flowers, too—how rich they are in scent here! how brilliant in colour! how magnificent in size! Wallflowers perfuming every street, and even every passage, while pinks and single carnations grow beside them, with no more soil than they require themselves; and from the tops of houses, where you least expect it, an aromatic flavour highly gratifying is diffused. The jessamine is large, broad-leaved, and beautiful as an orange-flower; but I have seen no roses equal to those at Lichfield, where on one tree I recollect counting eighty-four within my own reach; it grew against the house of Dr. Darwin. Such a profusion of sweets made me inquire yesterday morning for some scented pomatum, and they brought me accordingly one pot smelling strong of garden mint, the other of rue and tansy.

Thus do the inhabitants of every place forfeit or fling away those pleasures which the inhabitants of another place think they would use in a much wiser manner, had Providence bestowed the blessing upon them.

A young Milanese once, whom I met in London, saw me treat a hatter that lives in Pall Mall with the respect due to his merit. When the man was gone:

'Pray, madam,' says the Italian, 'is this a *gran riccone?*'*

'He is, perhaps,' replied I, 'worth twenty or thirty thousand pounds. I do not know what ideas you annex to a *gran riccone.*'

'Oh santissima Vergine!' exclaims the youth,

* Heavy-pursed fellow.

's'avessi io mai settanta mila zecchini! non so pur troppo cosa ne farei; ma questo è chiaro—non venderei mai cappelli' (Oh dear me! had I once seventy thousand sequins in my pocket, I would—dear—I cannot think myself what I should do with them all; but this at least is certain, I would not sell hats).

June 24, 1785.

St. John the Baptist is the tutelary saint of this city, and upon this day, of course, all possible rejoicings are made. After attending Divine service in the morning, we were carried to a house whence we could conveniently see the procession pass by. It was not solemn and stately as that I saw at Bologna, neither was it gaudy and jocund like the show made at Venice upon St. George's Day, but consisted chiefly in vast, heavy pageants, or a sort of temporary building set on wheels, and drawn by oxen some, and some by horses; others carried upon things made not unlike a chairman's horse in London, and supported by men, while priests, in various coloured dresses, according to their several stations in the Church, and to distinguish the parishes, etc., to which they belong, follow singing in praise of the saint.

Here is much emulation showed, too, I am told,

in these countries, where religion makes the great and almost the sole amusement of men's lives—who shall make most figure on St. John the Baptist's Day, produce most music, and go to most expense. For all these purposes subscriptions are set on foot for ornamenting and venerating such a picture, statue, etc., which are then added to the procession by the managers, and called a Confraternity, in honour of the Blessed Virgin Mary, the Angel Raphael, or who comes in their heads.

The lady of the house where we went to partake the diversion was not wanting in her part; there could not be fewer than a hundred and fifty people assembled in her rooms, but not crowded as we should have been in England; for the apartments in Italy are all high and large, and run in suites like Wanstead House in Essex, or Devonshire House in London exactly, but larger still, and with immense balconies and windows, not sashes, which move all away and give good room and air. The ices, refreshments, etc., were all excellent in their kinds, and liberally dispensed. The lady seemed to do the honours of her house with perfect good-humour, and everybody being full-dressed, though so early in a morning, added much to the general effect of the whole.

Here I had the honour of being introduced to

Cardinal Corsini, who put me a little out of countenance by saying suddenly:

'Well, madam, you never saw one of us red-legged partridges before, I believe; but you are going to Rome, I hear, where you will find such fellows as me no rarities.'

The truth is, I had seen the amiable Prince d'Orini at Milan, who was a cardinal, and who had taken delight in showing me prodigious civilities. Nothing ever struck me more than his abrupt entrance one night at our house, when we had a little music, and everybody stood up the moment he appeared; the prince, however, walked forward to the harpsichord, and blessed my husband in a manner the most graceful and affecting, then sat the amusement out, and returned the next morning to breakfast with us, when he indulged us with two hours' conversation at least, adding the kindest and most pressing invitations to his country seat among the mountains of Brianza when we should return from our tour of Italy in the spring of 1786. Florence, therefore, was not the first place that showed me a cardinal.

In the afternoon we all looked out of our windows which faced the street—not mine, as they happily command a view of the river, the Cascine woods, etc.—and from them enjoyed a complete sight of an

Italian horse-race. For after the coaches have paraded up and down some time to show the equipages, liveries, etc., all have on a sudden notice to quit the scene of action, and all do quit it in such a manner as is surprising. The street is now covered with sawdust, and made fast at both ends; the starting-post is adorned with elegant booths, lined with red velvet, for the court and first nobility; at the other end a piece of tapestry is hung, to prevent the creatures from dashing their brains out when they reach the goal. Thousands and ten thousands of people on foot fill the course, that it is standing wonder to me still that numbers are not killed. The prizes are now exhibited to view, quite in the old classical style ; a piece of crimson damask for the winner perhaps, a small silver bason and ewer for the second, and so on, leaving no performer unrewarded. At last come out the *concurrenti* without riders, but with a narrow leathern strap hung across their backs, which has a lump of ivory fastened to the end of it, all set full of sharp spikes like a hedgehog, and this goads them along while galloping worse than any spurs could do, because the faster they run, the more this odd machine keeps jumping up and down and pricking their sides ridiculously enough; and it makes one laugh to see that some of them are provoked by it not to run at all, but set about plunging in order to rid themselves of the inconvenience, instead of driving forward to divert the mob, who leap and shout and caper with delight, and lash the laggers along with great indignation indeed, and with the most comical gestures. I never saw horses in so droll a state of degradation before, for they are all striped or spotted, or painted of some colour to distinguish them each from other; and nine or ten often start at a time, to the great danger of lookers-on, I think, but exceedingly to my entertainment, who have the comfort of Mrs. Greatheed's company,[1] and the advantage of seeing all safely from her well-situated *terreno*, or ground-floor.

The chariot-race was more splendid, but less diverting. This was performed in the piazza, or square, an unpaved, open place not bigger than Covent Garden, I believe, and the ground strangely uneven. The cars were light and elegant, one driver and two horses to each, the first very much upon the principle of the antique chariots described by old poets, and the last trapped showily in various colours, adapted to the carriages, that people might make their bets accordingly upon the pink, the blue, the green, etc. I was exceedingly amused with seeing what so completely revived all classic images, and seemed so little altered from the classic times.

Cavalier d'Elci, in reply to my expressions of delight, told me that the same spirit still subsisted exactly, but that, in order to prevent accidents arising from the disputants' endeavours to overturn or circumvent each other, it was now sunk into a mere appearance of contest; for that all the chariots belonged to one man, who would doubtless be careful enough that his coachmen should not go to sparring at the hazard of their horses. The farce was carried on to the end, however, and the winner spread his velvet in triumph and drove round the course to enjoy the acclamations and caresses of the crowd.

We had another and another just such a race for three or four evenings together, and they got an English cock-tailed nag and set him to the business, as they said he was trained to it; but I don't recollect his making a more brilliant figure than his painted and chalked neighbours of the Continent.

We will not be prejudiced, however; that the Florentines know how to manage horses is certain, if they would take the trouble. Last night's theatre exhibited a proof of skill which might shame Astley and all his rivals. Count Pazzi having been prevailed on to lend his four beautiful chestnut favourites from his own carriage to draw a pageant upon the stage, I saw them yesterday evening harnessed all abreast, their own master in a dancer's habit, I was told, guiding them himself and personating the Cid, which was the name of the ballet, if I remember right, making his horses go clear round the stage, and turning at the lamps of the orchestra with such dexterity, docility and grace, that they seemed rather to enjoy than feel disturbance at the deafening noise of instruments, the repeated bursts of applause, and hollow sound of their own hoofs upon the boards of a theatre. I had no notion of such discipline, and thought the praises, though very loud, not ill-bestowed, as it is surely one of man's earliest privileges to replenish the earth with animal life and to subdue it.

I have for my own part, generally speaking, little delight in the obstreperous clamours of these heroic pantomimes; their battles are so noisy, and the acclamations of the spectators so distressing to weak nerves, I dread an Italian theatre—it distracts me. And always the same thing so, every and every night! how tedious it is!

This want of variety in the common pleasures of Italy though, and that surprising content with which a nation so sprightly looks on the same stuff and laughs at the same joke for months and months together, is perhaps less despicable to a thinking mind than the affectation of weariness and disgust where probably it is not felt at all, and where a gay heart often lurks under a clouded countenance, put on to deceive spectators into a notion of his philosophy who wears it, and, what is worse, who wears it chiefly as a mark of distinction cheaply obtained; for neither science, wit, nor courage are now found necessary to form a man of fashion.

In Italy, so far at least as I have gone, there is no impertinent desire of appearing what one is not—no searching for talk, and torturing expression to vary its phrases with something new and something fine; or else sinking into silence from despair of diverting the company, and, taking up the opposite method, contriving to impress them with an idea of bright intelligence concealed by modest doubts of our own powers and stifled by deep thought upon abstruse and difficult topics. To get quit of all these deep-laid systems of enjoyment, where

> 'To take our breakfast we project a scheme,
> Nor drink our tea without a stratagem,'

like the lady in Dr. Young, the surest method is to drop into Italy, where a conversazione at Venice or Florence, after the society of London, or *les petits soupers de Paris*, where, in their own phrase, un tableau n'attend pas l'autre,* is like taking a walk in Ilam Gardens or the Leasowes, after les parterres de Versailles ed i Terrazzi di Genoa. We are affected in the house, but natural in the gardens. Italians are natural in society, affected and constrained in the disposition of their grounds. No one, however, is good or bad, or wise or foolish, without a reason why. Restraint is made for man, and where religious and political liberty is enjoyed to its full extent, as in Great Britain, the people will forge shackles for themselves and lay the yoke heavy on society, to which, on the contrary, Italians give a loose, as compensation for their want of freedom in affairs of church or state.

I was observing that restraint was necessary to man; I have now learned a notion that noise is necessary too. The clatter made here in the Piazza del Duomo—where you sit in your carriage at a coffee-house door and chat with your friends according to Italian custom, while one eats ice and another calls for lemonade, to while away the time after dinner—the noise made then and there, I say, is beyond endurance.

Our Florentines have nothing on earth to do; yet a dozen fellows crying 'ciambelli!' (little cakes)

---

* One picture don't wait for another.

about the square, assisted by beggars, who lie upon the church steps and pray, or, rather, promise to pray, as loud as their lungs will let them, for the anime sante di purgatorio;* ballad-singers meantime endeavouring to drown these clamours in their own, and gentlemen's servants disputing at the doors whose master shall be first served, ripping up the pedigrees of each to prove superior claims for a biscuit or macaroon—do make such an intolerable clatter among them, that one cannot for one's life hear one another speak; and I did say just now that it were as good live at Brest or Portsmouth when the rival fleets were fitting out, as here, where real tranquillity subsists under a bustle merely imaginary. Our Grand Duke lives with little state, for aught I can observe here; but where there is least pomp there is commonly most power; for a man must have something *pour se dedommager*,† as the French express it, and this gentleman, possessing the *solide*, has no care for the *clinquant*, I trow. He tells his subjects when to go to bed, and who to dance with till the hour he chooses they should retire to rest, with exactly that sort of old-fashioned paternal authority that fathers used to exercise over their families in England before commerce had run

* Holy souls in purgatory.
† To make himself amends.

her levelling plough over all ranks and annihilated even the name of subordination. If he hear of any person living long in Florence without being able to give a good account of his business there, the Duke warns him to go away, and, if he loiter after such warning given, sends him out. Does any nobleman shine in pompous equipage or splendid table, the Grand Duke inquires soon into his pretensions, and scruples not to give personal advice and add grave reproofs with regard to the management of each individual's private affairs, the establishment of their sons, marriage of their sisters, etc. When they appeared to complain of this behaviour to me, 'I know not,' replied I, 'what to answer. One has always read and heard that the sovereigns ought to behave in despotic governments like the fathers of their family, and the Archbishop of Cambray inculcates no other conduct than this when advising his pupil, heir to the crown of France.'

'Yes, madam,' replied one of my auditors, with an acuteness truly Italian, ' but this prince is our father-in-law.'

The truth is, much of an English traveller's pleasure is taken off at Florence by the incessant complaints of a government he does not understand, and of oppressions he cannot remedy. 'Tis so dull to hear people lament the want of liberty, to which I question whether they have any pretensions, and without ever knowing whether it is the tyranny or the tyrant they complain of. Tedious, however, and most uninteresting are their accounts of grievances, which a subject of Great Britain has much ado to comprehend, and more to pity; as they are now all heart-broken because they must say their prayers in their own language, and not in Latin, which how it can be construed into misfortune a Tuscan alone can tell.

Lord Cork has given us many pleasing anecdotes of those who were formerly princes in this land. Had they a sovereign of the old Medici family, they would go to bed when he bid them quietly enough, I believe, and say their prayers in what language he would have them. 'Tis, in our parliamentary phrase, the men, not the measures, that offend them; and, while they pretend to whine as if despotism displeased them, they detest every republican state, feel envy towards Venice, and contempt for Lucca.

I have been out to dinner in the country near Prato, and what a charming—what a delightful thing is a nobleman's seat near Florence! How cheerful the society! how splendid the climate! how wonderful the prospects in this glorious country! The Arno rolling before his house, the

Apennines rising behind it!—a sight of fertility enjoyed by its inhabitants, and a view of such defences to their property, as Nature alone can bestow.

A peasantry so rich, too, that the wives and daughters of the farmer go dressed in jewels, and those of no small value. A pair of one-drop earrings, a broadish necklace, with a long piece hanging down the bosom and terminated with a cross, all of set garnets clear and perfect, is a common, a very common treasure to the females about this country; and on every Sunday or holiday, when they dress and mean to look pretty, their elegantly-disposed ornaments attract attention strongly, though I do not think them as handsome as the Lombard lasses, and our Venetian friends protest that the farmers at Crema in their state are still richer.

La Contadinella Toscana, however, in a very rich white silk petticoat, exceedingly full and short, to show her neat pink slipper and pretty ankle, her pink *corps de robe* and straps, with white silk lacing down the stomacher, puffed shift-sleeves, with heavy lace robbins ending at the elbow and fastened at the shoulders with at least eight or nine bows of narrow pink ribbon, a lawn handkerchief trimmed with broad lace, put on somewhat coquettishly and finishing in front with a nosegay—must make a lovely figure, at any rate, though the hair is drawn away from the face in a way rather too tight to be becoming, under a red velvet cushion edged with gold, which helps to wear it off, I think, but gives the small Leghorn hat, lined with green, a pretty perking air which is infinitely nymphish and smart. A tolerably pretty girl so dressed may surely more than vie with a *fille d'opéra* upon the Paris stage, even were she not set off, as these are, with a very rich suite of pearls or set garnets, that in France or England would not be purchased for less than forty or fifty pounds; and I am now speaking of the women perpetually under one's eye, not one or two picked from the crowd, like Mrs. Vanini, an innkeeper's wife in Florence, who, when she was dressed for the masquerade two nights ago, submitted her finery to Mrs. Greatheed's inspection and my own, who agreed she could not be so adorned in England for less than a thousand pounds.

It is true the nobility are proud of letting you see how comfortably their dependents live in Tuscany, but can any pride be more rational or generous, or any desire more patriotic? Oh, may they never look with less delight on the happiness of their inferiors, and then they will not murmur at their prince, whose protection of this rank among his subjects is eminently tender and attentive.

I have been showed, at the horse-race, the theatre, etc., the unfortunate grandson of King James II. He goes much into public still, though old and sickly, gives the English arms and livery, and wears the garter, which he has likewise bestowed upon his natural daughter. The Princess of Stoldberg, his consort, whom he always called queen, has left him to end a life of disappointment and sorrow by himself, with the sad reflection that even conjugal attachment, and of course domestic comfort, was denied to him, and fled—in defiance of poetry and fiction—fled with the crown to its powerful and triumphant possessors.

The states of Italy, being all under different rulers, are kept separate from each other, and speak a different dialect—that of Milan full of consonants and harsh to the ear, but abounding with classical expressions that rejoice one's heart and fill one with the oddest but most pleasing sensations imaginable. I heard a lady there call a runaway nobleman 'profugo' mighty prettily, and added that his conduct had put all the town into 'orgasmo grande.' All this, however, the Tuscans may possibly have in common with them. My knowledge of the language must remain ever too imperfect for me to depend on my own skill in it; all I can assert is, that the Florentines appear, as far as I have been competent to observe, to depend more on their own copious and beautiful language for expression than the Milanese do, who run to Spanish, Greek, or Latin for assistance, while half their tongue is avowedly borrowed from the French, whose pronunciation in the letter *u* they even profess to retain.

At Venice the sweetness of the patois is irresistible; their lips, incapable of uttering any but the sweetest sounds, reject all consonants they can get quit of, and make their mouths drop honey more completely than it can be said by any eloquence less mellifluous than their own.

The Bolognese dialect is detested by the other Italians as gross and disagreeable in its sounds; but every nation has the good word of its own inhabitants, and the language which Abbate Bianconi praises as nervous and expressive, I would advise no person less learned than himself to censure as disgusting or condemn as dull. I stayed very little at Bologna, saw nothing but their pictures, and heard nothing but their prayers; those were superior, I fancy, to all rivals. Language can be never spoken of by a foreigner to any effect of conviction. I have heard our countryman, Mr. Greatheed himself, who perhaps possesses more Italian than almost any Englishman, and studies it more closely, refuse to decide in critical disputations among his literary friends here, though the sonnets he writes in the Tuscan language are praised by the natives, who best understand it, and have been by some of them preferred to those written by Milton himself. Meantime, this is acknowledged to be the prime city for purity of phrase and delicacy of expression, which at last is so disguised to me by the guttural manner in which many sounds are pronounced, that I feel half-weary of running about from town to town so, and never arriving at any where I can understand the conversation without putting all the attention possible to their discourse. I am now told that less efforts will be necessary at Rome.

Nothing can be prettier, however, than the slow and tranquil manners of a Florentine, nothing more polished than his general address and behaviour—ever in the third person, though to a blackguard in the street, if he has not the honour of his particular acquaintance; while intimacy produces *voi* in those of the highest rank, who call one another Carlo and Angelo very sweetly, the ladies taking up the same notion, and saying Louisa or Maddalena without any addition at all.

The Don and Donna of Milan were offensive to me somehow, as they conveyed an idea of Spain, not Italy. Here Signora is the term, which better pleases one's ear, and Signora Contessa, Signora Principessa, if the person is of higher quality, resembles our manners more when we say 'my Lady Duchess,' etc. What strikes me as most observable is the uniformity of style in all the great towns.

At Venice the men of literature and fashion speak with the same accent, and, I believe, the same quick turns of expression as their gondolier; and the coachman of Milan talks no broader than the countess, who, if she does not speak always in French to a foreigner, as she would willingly do, tries in vain to talk Italian, and having asked you thus 'Alla capi?'—which means 'Ha ella capita?'—laughs at herself for trying to 'toscaneggiare,' as she calls it, and gives the point up with 'no cor altr,' that comes in at the end of every sentence, and means 'non occorre altro' (there is no more occurs upon the subject).

The laquais de place who attended us at Bologna was one of the few persons I had met with who spoke a language perfectly intelligible to me.

'Are you a Florentine, pray, friend?' said I.

'No, madam; but the combinations of this world having led me to talk much with strangers, I contrive to tuscanize it all I can for their advantage, and doubt not but it will tend to my own at last.'

Such a sentiment, so expressed by a footman, would set a plain man in London a-laughing, and make a fanciful lady imagine he was a nobleman disguised. Here nobody laughs, nor nobody stares nor wonders that their valet speaks just as good language or utters as well-turned sentences as themselves. Their cold answer to my amazement is as comical as the fellow's fine style. 'È battizzato,'* say they, 'come noi altri.'† But we are called away to hear the fair Fantastici, a young woman who makes improviso verses, and sings them, as they tell me, with infinite learning and taste. She is successor to the celebrated Corilla, who no longer exhibits the power she once held without a rival; yet to her conversations everyone still strives for admittance, though she is now ill and old and hoarse with repeated colds. She spares, however, now by no labour or fatigue to obtain and keep that superiority and admiration which one day perhaps gave her almost equal trouble to receive and to repay. But who can bear to lay their laurels by? Corilla is gay by nature, and witty, if I may say so, by habit; replete with fancy, and powerful to combine images apparently distant. Mankind is at last more just to people of talents than is universally allowed, I think. Corilla, without pretensions either to immaculate

* He has been baptized.   † As well as we.

character (in the English sense), deep erudition, or high birth, which an Italian esteems above all earthly things, has so made her way in the world, that all the nobility of both sexes crowd to her house, that no prince passes through Florence without waiting on Corilla, that the Capitol will long recollect her being crowned there, and that many sovereigns have not only sought her company, but have been obliged to put up with slights from her independent spirit, and from her airy, rather than haughty, behaviour. She is, however (I cannot guess why), not rich, and keeps no carriage; but, enjoying all the effect of money, convenience, company, and general attention, is probably very happy, as she does not much suffer her thoughts of the next world to disturb her felicity in this, I believe, while willing to turn everything into mirth and make all admire her wit, even at the expense of their own virtue. The following epigram, made by her, will explain my meaning, and give a specimen of her present powers of improvisation, undecayed by ill-health, and I might add undismayed by it. An old gentleman here, one Gaetano Testa Grossa, had a young wife, whose name was Mary, and who brought him a son when he was more than seventy years old. Corilla led him gaily into the circle of company with these words :

'Miei Signori, Io vi presento
    Il buon Uomo Gaetano ;
  Che non sà che cosa sia
    Il misterio sovr' umano
  Del Figliuolo di Maria.'

We were a-walking last night in the gardens of Porto St. Gallo, and met two or three well-looking women of the second rank, with a baby, four or five years old at most, dressed in the habit of a Dominican friar, bestowing the benediction as he walked along like an officiating priest. I felt a shock given to all my nerves at once, and asked Cavalier d'Elci the meaning of so strange a device. His reply to me was, 'È divozione mal intesa, signora;'* and turning round to the other gentlemen : 'Now, this folly,' said he, 'a hundred years ago would have been the object of profound veneration and prodigious applause. Fifty years hence it would be censured as hypocritical ; it is now passed by wholly unnoticed, except by this foreign lady, who, I believe, thought it was done for a joke.'

But I must bid adieu to beautiful Florence, where the streets are kept so clean one is afraid to dirty them, and not one's self, by walking in them ; where the public walks are all nicely weeded, as in England, and the gardens have a homish and Bath-like look

---

* ''Tis ill-understood devotion, madam.'

that is excessively cheering to an English eye; where, when I dined at Prince Corsini's table, I heard the cardinal say grace, and thought of the ceremonies at Queen's College, Oxford; where I had the honour of entertaining, at my own dinner on the 25th of July, many of the Tuscan and many of the English nobility, and Nardini kindly played a solo in the evening at a concert we gave in Meghitt's great room; where we have compiled the little book amongst us, known by the name of the 'Florence Miscellany,' as a memorial of that friendship which does me so much honour, and which I earnestly hope may long subsist among us; where, in short, we have lived exceeding comfortably, but where dear Mrs. Greatheed and myself have encouraged each other in saying it would be particularly sad to die, not of the gnats, or more properly mosquitoes— for they do not sting one quite to death, though their venom has swelled my arm so as to oblige me to carry it for this last week in a sling—but of the *mal di petto*, which is endemial in this country, and much resembling our pleurisy in its effects.

Blindness, too, seems no uncommon misfortune at Florence, from the strong reverberation of the sun's rays on houses of the cleanest and most brilliant whiteness—kept so elegantly nice, too, that I should despair of seeing more delicacy at Amsterdam.

Apoplexies are likewise frequent enough. I saw a man carried out stone dead from St. Pancrazio's Church one morning about noonday, but nobody seemed disturbed at the event, I think, except myself. Though this is no good town to take one's last leave of life in, neither, as the body one has been so long taking care of would in twenty-four hours be hoisted up upon a common cart, with those of all the people who died the same day, and, being fairly carried out of Porto San Gallo towards the dusk of evening, would be shot into a hole dug away from the city, properly enough, to protect Florence and keep it clear of putrid disorders and disagreeable smells. All this with little ceremony, to be sure, and less distinction; for the Grand Duke suffers the pride of birth to last no longer than life, however, and demolishes every hope of the woman of quality lying in a separate grave from the distressed object who begged at her carriage-door when she was last on an airing.

Let me add that his liberality of sentiment extends to virtue on the one hand, if hardness of heart may be complained of on the other. He suffers no difference of opinions to operate on his philosophy, and I believe we heretics here should sleep among the best of his Tuscan nobles. But there is no comfort in the possibility of being buried alive by the excessive haste with which people are catched up and hurried away, before it can be known almost whether all sparks of life are extinct or no.

Of elegant Florence, then, so ornamented and so lovely, so neat that it is said she should be seen only on holidays; dedicated of old to Flora, and still the residence of sweetness, grace, and the fine arts particularly; of these kind friends, too, so amiable, so hospitable, where I had the choice of four boxes every night at the theatre, and a certainty of charming society in each, we must at last unwillingly take leave, and on to-morrow, the twelfth day of September, 1785, once more commit ourselves to our coach, which has hitherto met with no accident that could affect us, and in which, with God's protection, I fear not my journey through what is left of Italy, though such tremendous tales are told in many of our travelling books of terrible roads and wicked postillions, and ladies labouring through the mire on foot, to arrive at bad inns where nothing eatable could be found.

CHAPTER VII

LUCCA, LEGHORN, BATHS OF PISA, SIENA

Lucca—A Tiny Republic—Black Dresses—Absence of Crime—Peasant Dresses—Merry Idleness—Leghorn—Resemblance to an English Seaport—Varied Costumes—Tuscan Feebleness—A Protestant Cemetery—Baths of Pisa—Beautiful Scenery—Vernun—A Thunderstorm—Siena—Sweetness of Language.

Lucca.

FROM the head-quarters of painting, sculpture, and architecture, then, where art is at her acme, and from a people polished into brilliancy, perhaps a little into weakness, we drove through the celebrated vale of Arno, thick hedges on each side us, which in spring must have been covered with blossoms and fragrant with perfume, now loaded with uncultivated fruits—the wild grape, raspberry, and azaroli—inviting to every sense and promising every joy. This beautiful and fertile, this highly-adorned and truly delicious country carried us forward to Lucca, where the panther sits at the gate, and liberty is written up on every wall and door. It is so long since I have seen the word that even the letters of it rejoice my heart; but how the panther came to be its emblem, who can tell? Unless the philosophy we learn from old Lilly in our childhood were true—nec vult panthera domari.*

That this fairy commonwealth should so long have maintained its independency is strange; but Howel attributes her freedom to the active and industrious spirit of the inhabitants, who, he says, resemble a hive of bees for order and for diligence. I never did see a place so populous for the size of it; one is actually thronged running up and down the streets of Lucca, though it is a little town enough for a capital city, to be sure—larger than Salisbury, though, and prettier than Nottingham, the beauties of both which places it unites with all the charms peculiar to itself.

The territory they claim, and of which no power dares attempt to dispossess them, is much about the size of Rutlandshire, I fancy, surrounded and apparently fenced in on every side by the Apennines as by a wall—that wall a hot one on the southern side, and wholly planted over with vines—while the soft shadows which fall upon the declivity of the mountains make it inexpressibly pretty, and form, by the particular disposition of their light and shadow,

* That the panther will never be tamed.

a variety which no other prospect so confined can possibly enjoy.

This is the Ilam Gardens of Europe, and whoever has seen that singular spot in Derbyshire, belonging to Mr. Port, has seen little Lucca in a convex mirror. Some writer calls it a ring upon the finger of the Emperor, under whose protection it has been hitherto preserved safe from the Grand Duke of Tuscany till these days, in which the interests of those two sovereigns, united by intimacy as by blood and resemblance of character, are become almost exactly the same.

A Doge, whom they call the Principe, is elected every two months, and is assisted by ten senators in the administration of justice.

Their armoury is the prettiest plaything I ever yet saw, neatly kept, and capable of furnishing twenty-five thousand men with arms. Their revenues are about equal to the Duke of Bedford's, I believe— eighty or eighty-five thousand pounds sterling a-year – every spot of ground belonging to these people being cultivated to the highest pitch of perfection that agriculture, or, rather, gardening (for one cannot call these enclosures fields), will admit; and, though it is holiday-time just now, I see no neglect of necessary duty. They were watering away this morning at seven o'clock, just as we do in a nursery-ground about London, a hundred men at once, or more, before they came home to make themselves smart and go to hear music in their best church in honour of some saint, I have forgotten who; but he is the patron of Lucca, and cannot be accused of neglecting his charge, that is certain.

This city seems really under admirable regulations. Here are fewer beggars than even at Florence, where, however, one for fifty in the states of Genoa or Venice do not meet your eyes; and either the word liberty has bewitched me, or I see an air of plenty without insolence, and business without noise, that greatly delight me. Here is much cheerfulness, too, and gay good humour; but this is the season of devotion at Lucca, and in these countries the ideas of devotion and diversion are so blended, that all religious worship seems connected with, and to me now regularly implies, a festive show.

Well, as the Italians say, 'Il mondo è bello perche è variabile.'* We English dress our clergymen in black, and go ourselves to the theatre in colours. Here matters are reversed; the church at noon looked like a flower-garden, so gaily adorned were the priests, confrairies, etc., while the Opera-house at night had more the air of a funeral, as everybody was dressed in black, a circumstance I had forgotten

* 'The world is pleasant because it is various.'

the meaning of, till reminded that such was once the emulation of finery among the persons of fashion in this city, that it was found convenient to restrain the spirit of expense by obliging them to wear constant mourning, a very rational and well-devised rule in a town so small, where everybody is known to everybody, and where, when this silly excitement to envy is wisely removed, I know not what should hinder the inhabitants from living like those one reads of in the Golden Age, which, above all others, this climate most resembles, where pleasure contributes to soothe life, commerce to quicken it, and faith extends its prospects to eternity. Such is, or such at least appears to me, this lovely territory of Lucca—where cheap living, free government, and genteel society may be enjoyed with a tranquillity unknown to larger states; where there are delicious and salutary baths a few miles out of town, for the nobility to make *villeggiatura* at; and where, if those nobility were at all disposed to cultivate and communicate learning, every opportunity for study is afforded.

Some drawbacks will, however, always be found from human felicity. I once mentioned this place with warm expectations of delight to a Milanese lady of extensive knowledge and every elegant accomplishment worthy her high birth, the Contessa Melzi Resta.

'Why, yes,' said she, 'if you would find out the place where common-sense stagnates, and every topic of conversation dwindles and perishes away by too frequent or too unskilful touching and handling, you must go to Lucca. My ill-health sent me to their beautiful baths one summer, where all the faculties of my body were restored, thank God, but those of my soul were stupefied to such a degree, that at last I was fit to keep no other company but *Dame Lucchesi*, I think; and our talk was soon ended, heaven knows, for when they had once asked me of an evening what I had for dinner, and told me how many pair of stockings their neighbours sent to the wash, we had done.'

This was a young, a charming, a lively lady of quality, full of curiosity to know the world, and of spirits to bustle through it; but had she been battered through the various societies of London and Paris for eighteen or twenty years together, she would have loved Lucca better and despised it less. 'We must not look for whales in the Euxine Sea,' says an old writer, and we must not look for great men or great things in little nations, to be sure: but let us respect the innocence of childhood, and regard with tenderness the territory of Lucca, where no man has been murdered during the life or memory of any of its peaceful inhabitants; where one robbery alone has been committed for sixteen years, and the thief hanged by a Florentine executioner borrowed for the purpose, no Lucchese being able or willing to undertake so horrible an office, with terrifying circumstances of penitence and public reprehension; where the governed are so few in proportion to the governors, all power being circulated among four hundred and fifty nobles, and the whole country producing scarcely ninety thousand souls. A great boarding-school in England is really an infinitely more licentious place, and grosser immoralities are every day connived at in it than are known to pollute this delicate and curious commonwealth, which keeps a council always subsisting, called the Discoli, to examine the lives and conduct, professions, and even health of their subjects; and once o' year they sweep the town of vagabonds, which till then are caught up and detained in a house of correction, and made to work, if not disabled by lameness, till the hour of their release and dismission. I wondered there were so few beggars about, but the reason is now apparent; these we see are neighbours, come hither only for the three days' gala.

I was wonderfully solicitous to obtain some of their coin, which carries on it the image of no earthly prince, but His head only who came to redeem us from general slavery on the one side, Jesus Christ; on the other the word 'Libertas.'

Our peasant girls here are in a new dress to me; no more jewels to be seen, no more pearls, the finery of which so dazzled me in Tuscany: these wenches are prohibited such ornaments, it seems. A muslin handkerchief, folded in a most becoming manner and starched exactly enough to make it wear clean four days, is the head-dress of Lucchese lasses; it is put on turban-wise, and they button their gowns close, with long sleeves *à la Savoyarde;* but it is made often of a stiff brocaded silk, and green lapels, with cuffs of the same colour; nor do they wear any hats at all to defend them from a sun which does undoubtedly mature the fig and ripen the vine, but which, by the same excess of power, exalts the venom of the viper, and gives the scorpion means to keep me in perpetual torture for fear of his poison, of which, though they assure us death is seldom the consequence among them, I know his sting would finish me at once, because the gnats at Florence were sufficient to lame me for a considerable time.

The dialect has lost much of the guttural sound that hurt one's ear at the last place of residence; but here is an odd squeaking accent, that distinguishes the Tuscan of Lucca.

The place appropriated for airing, showing fine

equipages, etc., is beautiful beyond all telling, from the peculiar shadows on the mountains. They make the bastions of the town their Corso, but none except the nobles can go and drive upon one part of it. I know not how many yards of ground is thus set apart sacred to sovereignty, but it makes one laugh.

Our inn here is an excellent one, as far as I am concerned; and the salad-oil, green like Irish usquebaugh, nothing was ever so excellent. I asked the French valet who dresses our hair, 'Si ce n'etait pas une république mignonne?'*

'Ma foi, madame, je la trouve plus tôt la république des rats et des souris,'† replies the fellow, who had not slept all night, I afterwards understood, for the noise those troublesome animals made in his room.

Pisa.

The battle of the bridge here at Pisa drew a great many spectators this year, as it has not been performed for a considerable time before; the waiters at our inn here give a better account of it than one should have got perhaps from cavalier or dama, who would have felt less interested in the business and seen it from a greater distance. The armies of

* 'If it were not a dear little pretty commonwealth, this?'
† 'Faith, madam, I call it the republic of the rats and mice.'

Sant' Antonio, and I think San Giovanni Battista, but I will not be positive as to the last, disputed the possession of the bridge, and fought gallantly, I fancy; but the first remained conqueror, as our very conversible Camerieres took care to inform us, as it was on that side it seems that they had exerted their valour.

Calling theatres and ships and running horses and mock fights, and almost everything so by the names of saints, whom we venerate in silence and they themselves publicly worship, has a most profane and offensive sound with it, to be sure, and shocks delicate ears very dreadfully; and I used to reprimand my maids at Milan for bringing up the blessed Virgin Mary's name on every trivial, almost on every ludicrous occasion, with a degree of sharpness they were not accustomed to, because it kept me in a constant shivering. Yet let us reflect a moment on our own conduct in England, and we shall be forced candidly to confess that the Puritans alone keep their lips unpolluted by breach of the third commandment, while the common exclamation of 'Good God!' scrupled by few people on the slightest occurrences, and apparently without any temptation in the world, is no less than gross irreverence of His sacred name.

The misery of Tuscany is, that all animals thrive so happily under this productive sun, so that, if you scorn the *Zanzariere,* you are half-devoured before morning, and so disfigured that I defy one's nearest friends to recollect one's countenance; while the spiders sting as much as any of their insects, and one of them bit me this very day till the blood came.

With all this not ill-founded complaint of these our active companions, my constant wonder is that the grapes hang untouched this 20th of September, in vast heavy clusters covered with bloom, and unmolested by insects, which, with a quarter of this heat in England, are encouraged to destroy all our fruit, in spite of the gardener's diligence to blow up nests, cover the walls with netting, and hang them about with bottles of syrup to court the creatures in, who otherwise so damage every fig and grape and plum of ours, that nothing but the skins are left remaining by now. Here no such contrivances are either wanted or thought on, and, while our islanders are sedulously bent to guard, and studious to invent new devices to protect their half-dozen peaches from their half-dozen wasps, the standard trees of Italy are loaded with high-flavoured and delicious fruits.

The roadside is indeed hedged with festoons of

vines, crawling from olive to olive, which they plant in the ditches of Tuscany as we do willows in Britain; mulberry-trees, too, by the thousand, and some pollarded poplars serve for support to the glorious grapes that will now soon be gathered. What least contributes to the beauty of the country, however, is perhaps most subservient to its profits. I am ashamed to write down the returns of money gained by the oil alone in this territory and that of Lucca, where I was much struck with the colour as well as the excellence of this useful commodity. Nor can I tell why none of that green cast comes over to England, unless it is that, like essential oil of camomile, it loses the tint by exposure to the air.

An olive-tree, however, is no elegantly-growing or happily-coloured plant; straggling and dusky, one is forced to think of its produce before one can be pleased with its merits, as in a deformed and ugly friend or companion.

The fogs now begin to fall pretty heavily in a morning, and, rising about the middle of the day, leave the sun at liberty to exert his violence very powerfully. At night come forth the inhabitants, like dor-beetles at sunset on the coast of Sussex; then is their season to walk and chat, and sing and make love, and run about the street with a girl and a guitar, to eat ice and drink lemonade, but never to be seen drunk or quarrelsome or riotous. Though night is the true season of Italian felicity, they place not their happiness in brutal frolics any more than in malicious titterings·; they are idle, and they are merry; it is, I think, the worst we can say of them. They are idle because there is little for them to do, and merry because they have little given them to think about. To the busy Englishman they might well apply these verses of his own Milton in the Masque of Comus :

> 'What have we with day to do?
> Sons of Care ! 'twas made for you.'

Leghorn.

Here we are by the sea-side once more—in a trading town, too—and I should think myself in England almost, but for the difference of dresses that pass under my balcony; for here we were immediately addressed by a young English gentleman, who politely put us in possession of his apartments, the best situated in the town ; and with him we talked of the dear coast of Devonshire, agreed upon the resemblance between that and these environs, but gave the preference to home on account of its undulated shore, finely fringed with woodlands, which here are wanting ; nor is this verdure equal to ours in vivid colouring, or variegated with so much taste as those lovely hills which are adorned by the antiquities of Powderham Castle and the fine disposition of Lord Lisburne's park.

But here is an English consul at Leghorn. Yes, indeed! an English chapel, too, our own king's arms over the door, and in the desk and pulpit an English clergyman, high in character, eminent for learning, genteel in his address, and charitable in every sense of the word—as such, truly loved and honoured by those of his own persuasion, exceedingly respected by those of every other which fill this extraordinary city—a place so populous that Cheapside alone can surpass it.

It is not a large place, however; one very long, straight street, and one very large, wide square, not less than Lincoln's Inn Fields, but I think bigger, form the whole of Leghorn; which I can compare to nothing but a camera obscura, or magic lantern, exhibiting prodigious variety of different, and not uninteresting, figures, that pass and repass to my incessant delight, and give that sort of empty amusement which is 'à la portée de chacun'* so completely, that for the present it really serves to drive everything else from my head, and makes me little desirous to quit for any other diversion the windows or balcony, whence I look down now upon a Levan-

* Within everyone's reach.

tine Jew, dressed in long robes, a sort of odd turban, and immense beard; now upon a Tuscan contadinella, with the little straw hat, nosegay and jewels I have been so often struck with. Here an Armenian Christian, with long hair, long gown, long beard, all black as a raven, who calls upon an old, gray Franciscan friar for a walk; while a Greek woman, obliged to cross the street on some occasion, throws a vast white veil all over her person, lest she should undergo the disgrace of being seen at all.

Sometimes a group goes by, composed of a broad Dutch sailor, a dry-starched Puritan, and an old French officer, whose knowledge of the world and habitual politeness contrive to conceal the contempt he has of his companions.

The *Contorni* of Leghorn are really very pretty; the Apennine mountains degenerate into hills as they run round the bay, but gain in beauty what in sublimity they lose.

To enjoy an open sea-view, one must drive further; and it really affords a noble prospect from that rising ground where I understand that the rich Jews hold their summer habitations. They have a synagogue in the town, where I went one evening and heard the Hebrew service, and thought of what Dr. Burney says of their singing.

It is, however, no credit to the Tuscans to tell, that of all the people gathered together here, they are the worst-looking—I speak of the men—but it is so. When compared with the German soldiery, the English sailors, the Venetian traders, the Neapolitan peasants—for I have seen some of them here—how feeble a fellow is a genuine Florentine! And when one recollects the cottagers of Lombardy—that handsome, hardy race, bright in their expression and muscular in their strength—it is still stranger what can have weakened these too delicate Tuscans so. As they are very rich, and might be very happy under the protection of a prince who lets slip no opportunity of preferring his plebeian to his patrician subjects; yet here at Leghorn they have a tender frame and an unhealthy look, occasioned possibly by the stagnant waters, which render the environs unwholesome enough, I believe, and the millions of live creatures they produce are enough to distract a person not accustomed to such buzzing company.

We went out for air yesterday morning three or four miles beyond the town-walls, where I looked steadily at the sea, till I half thought myself at home. The ocean being peculiarly British property favoured the idea, and for a moment I felt as if on our southern coast. We walked forward towards the shore, and I stepped upon some rocks that broke the waves as they rolled in, and was wishing for a good bathing-house that one might enjoy the benefit of salt water so long withheld, till I saw our laquais de place crossing himself at the carriage-door and wondering, as I afterwards found out, at my matchless intrepidity. The mind, however, took another train of thought, and we returned to the coach, which when we arrived at I refused to enter —not without screaming, I fear—as a vast hornet had taken possession in our absence, and the very notion of such a companion threw me into an agony. Our attendant's speech to the coachman, however, made me more than amends:

'Ora si vede, amico' (says he), 'cos' è la Donna; del mare istesso non hà paura, e pur và in convulsioni per via d' una mosca.'*

This truly Tuscan and highly contemptuous harangue, uttered with the utmost deliberation, and added to the absence of the hornet, sent me laughing into the carriage, with great esteem of our philosophical Rosso, for so the fellow was called because he had red hair.

Our evening's walk was directed towards the burying-ground appointed here to receive the bodies

* 'Now, my friend, do but observe what a thing is a woman! She is not afraid even of the roaring ocean, and yet goes into fits almost at the sight of a fly.'

of our countrymen, and consecrated according to the rites of the Anglican Church; for here, under protection of a factory, we enjoy that which is vainly sought for under the auspices of a king's ambassador. Here we have a churchyard of our own, and are not condemned, as at other towns in Italy, to be stuffed into a hole like dogs, after having spent our money among them like princes. Prejudice, however, is not banished from Leghorn, though convenience keeps all in good-humour with each other. The Italians fail not to class the subjects of Great Britain among the pagan inhabitants of the town, and, to distinguish themselves, say 'Noi altri Christiani.'* Their aversion to a Protestant, conceal it as they may, is ever implacable, and the last day only will convince them that it is criminal.

'Cœlum non animum mutant '† is an old observation; I passed this afternoon in confirming the truth of it among the English traders settled here, whose conversation, manners, ideas, and language were so truly Londonish, so little changed by transmigration, that I thought some enchantment had suddenly operated and carried me to drink tea in the regions of Bucklersbury.

Well, it is a great delight to see such a society

---

* 'We that are Christians.'
† 'One changes one's sky, but not one's soul.'

subsisting in Italy, after all, established where distress may run for refuge, and sickness retire to prepare for lasting repose; whence narrowness of mind is banished by principles of universal benevolence, and prejudice precluded by Christian charity; where the purse of the British merchant, ever open to the poor, is certain to succour and to soothe affliction ; and where it is agreed that more alms are given by the natives of our island alone than by all the rest of Leghorn and the palaces of Pisa put together.

Bagni di Pisa.

It was perhaps particularly delightful to me to obtain once more a cottage in the country, after running so from one great city to another, and for the first week I did nothing but rejoice in a solitude so new, so salutiferous, so total. I therefore begged my husband not to hurry us to Rome, but take the house we lived in for a longer term, as I would now play the English housewife in Italy, I said; and accordingly began calling the chickens and ducks under my window, tasted the new wine as it ran purple from the cask, caressed the meek oxen that drew it to our door, and felt sensations so unaffectedly pastoral that nothing in romance ever exceeded my felicity.

These springs are much frequented by the Court, I find, and here are very tolerable accommodations; but it is not the season now, and our solitude is perfect in a place which beggars all description, where the mountains are mountains of marble, and the bushes on them bushes of myrtle, large as our hawthorns and white with blossoms, as they are at the same time of year in Devonshire; where the waters are salubrious, the herbage odoriferous, every trodden step breathing immediate fragrance from the crushed sweets of thyme and marjoram and winter savoury; while the birds and the butterflies frolic around, and flutter among the loaded lemon and orange and olive trees, till imagination is fatigued with following the charms that surround one.

I am come home this moment from a long but not tedious walk among the crags of this glorious mountain, the base of which nearly reaches, within half a mile perhaps, to the territories of Lucca. Some country girls passed me with baskets of fruit, chickens, etc., on their heads. I addressed them as natives of the last-named place, saying I knew them to be such by their dress and air; one of them instantly replied:

'Oh sì, siamo Lucchesi, noi altri; già si può vedere subito una Reppublicana, e credo bene ch' ella se n' é accorta benissimo che siamo del paese della libertà.'*

I will add that these females wear no ornaments at all, are always proud and gay, and sometimes a little saucy too. The Tuscan damsels, loaded with gold and pearls, have a less assured look, and appear disconcerted when in company with their freer neighbours—let them tell why.

Meantime, my fairy dream of fantastic delight seems fading away apace. Mr. Piozzi has been ill, and of a putrid complaint in his throat, which above all things I should dread in this hot climate. This accident, assisted by other concurring circumstances, has convinced me that we are not shut up in measureless content, as Shakespeare calls it, even under St. Julian's Hill; for here was no help to be got, in the first place, except the useless conversation of a medical gentleman whose accent and language might have pleased a disengaged mind, but had little chance to tranquillize an affrighted one. What is worse, here was no rest to be had for the multitudes of vermin upstairs and below. When we first hired the house, I remember my maid jumping up on one of the kitchen chairs while a ragged lad cleared that apartment for her of scorpions, to the

* 'Oh yes, we are Lucca people, sure enough, and I am persuaded that you soon saw in our faces that we come from a land of liberty.'

number of seventeen. But now the biters and stingers drive me quite wild, because one must keep the windows open for air, and a sick man can enjoy none of that, being closed up in the *zanzariere* and obliged to respire the same breath over and over again, which, with a sore throat and fever, is most melancholy; but I keep it wet with vinegar, and defy the hornets how I can.

What is more surprising than all, however, is to hear that no lemons can be procured for less than twopence English a-piece; and now I am almost ready to join myself in the general cry against Italian imposition, and recollect the proverb which teaches us:

> 'Chi hà da far con Tosco,
> Non bisogna esser losco;'*

as I am confident they cannot be worth even twopence a hundred here, where they hang like apples in our cider countries; but the rogues know that my husband is sick, and upon poor me they have no mercy.

I have sent our folks out to gather fruit at a venture; and now this misery will soon be ended with his illness, driven away by deluges of lemonade, I think, made in defiance of wasps, flies, and a kind

---

* 'Who has to do with Tuscan wight,
Of both his eyes will need the light.'

of volant beetle, wonderfully beautiful and very pertinacious in his attacks, and who makes dreadful depredations on my sugar and currant jelly, so necessary on this · occasion of illness, and so attractive to all these detestable inhabitants of a place so lovely.

My patient, however, complaining that although I kept these harpies at a distance, no sleep could yet be obtained, I resolved, when he was risen and had changed his room, to examine into the true cause, and, with my maid's assistance, unripped the mattress, which was, without exaggeration or hyperbole, all alive with creatures wholly unknown to me. Nondescripts in nastiness I believe they are, like maggots with horns and tails—such a race as I never saw or heard of, and as would have disgusted Mr. Leeuenhoeck himself. My willingness to quit this place and its hundred-footed inhabitants was quickened three nights after by a thunderstorm, such as no dweller in more northern latitudes can form an idea of, which, assisted by some few slight shocks of an earthquake, frightened us all from our beds, sick and well, and gave me an opportunity of viewing such flashes of lightning as I had never contemplated till now, and such as it appeared impossible to escape from with life. The tremendous claps of thunder re-echoing among these

Apennines, which double every sound, were truly dreadful. I really and sincerely thought St. Julian's mountain was rent by one violent stroke, accompanied with a rough concussion, and that the rock would fall upon our heads by morning; while the agonies of my English maid and the French valet became equally insupportable to themselves and me, who could only repeat the same unheeded consolations, and protest our resolution of releasing them from this theatre of distraction the moment our departure should become practicable. Meantime, the rain fell, and such a torrent came tumbling down the sides of St. Juliano as I am persuaded no female courage could have calmly looked on. I therefore waited its abatement in a darkened room, packed up our coach without waiting to copy over the verses my admiration of the place had prompted, and drove forward to Siena, through Pisa again, where our friends told us of the damages done by the tempest, and showed us a pretty little church just out of town where the officiating priest at the altar was saved almost by miracle, as the lightning melted one of the chalices completely, and twisted the brazen-gilt crucifix quite round in a very astonishing manner.

Siena, 20th October, 1786.

We arrived here last night, having driven through the sweetest country in the world; and here are a few timber-trees at last, such as I have not seen for a long time, the Tuscan spirit of mutilation being so great that everything till now has been pollarded that would have passed twenty feet in height. This is done to support the vines, and not suffer their rambling produce to run out of the way and escape the gripe of the gatherers. I have eaten too many of these delicious grapes, however, and it is now my turn to be sick. No wonder; I know few who would resist a like temptation, especially as the inn afforded but a sorry dinner, whilst every hedge provided so noble a dessert. 'Passera pur la malattia,'* as these soft-mouthed people tell me—the sooner, perhaps, as we are not here annoyed by insects, which poison the pleasure of other places in Italy. Here are only lizards—lovely creatures!—who, being of a beautiful light green colour upon the back and legs, reside in whole families at the foot of every tree, and turn their scarlet bosoms to the sun, as if to display the glories of colouring which his beams alone can bestow.

The pleasing tales told of this pretty animal's

---

* 'The disorder will die away, though.'

amical disposition towards man are strictly true, I hear; and it is no longer ago than yesterday I was told an odd anecdote of a young farmer, who, carrying a basket of figs to his mistress, lay down in the field as he crossed it, quite overcome with the weather, and fell fast asleep. A serpent, attracted by the scent, twined round the basket, and would have bit the fellow as well as robbed him, had not a friendly lizard waked and given him warning of the danger.

Swift says that in the course of life he meets many asses, but they have not lucky names. I have met many vipers, and so few lizards, it is surprising! but they will not live in London.

All the stories one has ever heard of sweetness in language and delicacy in pronunciation fall short of Sienese converse. The girls who wait on us at the inn here would be treasures in England, could one get them thither, and they need move nothing but their tongues to make their fortunes. I told Rosetta so, and said I would steal from them a poor girl of eight years old, whom they kept out of charity and called Olympia, to be my language mistress.

'Battezzata com' è, la lascieremo Christiana,'* was the answer.

It is impossible, without their manners, to express

---

* 'Being baptized as she is, we will leave her a Christian.'

their elegance, their superior delicacy, graceful without diffusion and terse without laconicism. You ask the way to the town of a peasant girl, and she replies:

'Passato 'l Ponte, o pur barcato' l Fiume, eccola a Siena.'*

And as we drove towards the city in the evening, our postilion sung improviso verses on his sweetheart, a widow who lived down at Pistoja, they told me. I was ashamed to think that no desk or study was likely to have produced better on so trite a subject. Candour must confess, however, that no thought was new, though the language made them for a moment seem so.

This town is neat and cleanly, and comfortable and airy. The prospect from the public walks wants no beauty but water; and here is a suppressed convent on the neighbouring hill, where we half-longed to build a pretty cottage, as the ground is now to be disposed of vastly cheap, and half one's work is already done in the apartments once occupied by friars. With half a word's persuasion I should fix for life here. The air is so pure, the language so pleasing, the place so inviting—but we drive on.

* 'The bridge once passed, or the river crossed, Siena lies before you.'

CHAPTER VIII

ROME

The Strada del Popolo—Dislike of Perfumes—Fogs—Squalors—Crime —An Old Idol—A City of Statues.

THIS is the first town in Italy I have arrived at yet where the ladies fairly drive up and down a long street by way of showing their dress, equipages, etc., without even a pretence of taking fresh air. At Turin the view from the place destined to this amusement would tempt one out merely for its own sake, and at Milan they drive along a planted walk at least a stone's-throw beyond the gates. Bologna calls its serious inhabitants to a little rising ground, whence the prospect is luxuriantly verdant and smiling. The Lucca bastions are beyond all in a peculiar style of miniature beauty; and even the Florentines, though lazy enough, creep out to Porto St. Gallo. But here at Roma la Santa the street is all our Corso—a fine one doubtless, and called the Strada

ROME: THE PIAZZA DEL POPOLO.
From an Engraving by Vasi.

del Popolo with infinite propriety, for except in that strada there is little populousness enough, God knows. Twelve men to a woman even there, and as many ecclesiastics to a layman. All this, however, is fair, when celibacy is once enjoined as a duty in one profession, encouraged as a virtue in all. Where females are superfluous and half prohibited, it were foolish to complain of the decay of population.

'Au reste,' as the French say, we must not be too sure that all who dress like abates are such. Many gentlemen wear black as the Court garb, many because it is not costly, and many for reasons of mere convenience and dislike of change.

I see not here the attractive beauty which caught my eye at Venice; but the women at Rome have a most Juno-like carriage, and fill up one's idea of Livia and Agrippina well enough. The men have rounder faces than one sees in other towns, I think; bright, black, and somewhat prominent eyes, with the finest teeth in Europe. A story told me this morning struck my fancy much—of an herb-woman who kept a stall here in the market, and who, when the people ran out flocking to see the Queen of Naples as she passed, began exclaiming to her neighbours:

'Ah, povera Roma! tempo fù quando passò qui

prigioniera la regina Zenobia; altra cosa, amica, roba tutta diversa di questa reginuccia!"*

A characteristic speech enough; but in this town, unlike to every other, the things take my attention all away from the people, while in every other the people have had much more of my mind employed upon them than the things.

The music is not in a state so capital as we left it in the north of Italy; we regret Nardini of Florence, Alessandri of Venice, and Ronzi of Milan; and who that has heard Signor Marchesi sing could ever hear a successor (for rival he has none), without feeling total indifference to all their best endeavours?

The conversations of Cardinal de Bernis and Madame de' Boccapaduli are what my countrywomen talk most of; but the Roman ladies cannot endure perfumes, and faint away even at an artificial rose. I went but once among them, when Memmo, the Venetian ambassador, did me the honour to introduce me somewhere, but the conversation was soon over—not so my shame, when I perceived all the company shrink from me very oddly and stop their noses with rue, which a servant

* 'Ah, poor degraded Rome! time was, my dear, when the great Zenobia passed through these streets in chains; another guess figure from this little Queeney, in good time!'

brought to their assistance on open salvers. I was by this time more like to faint away than they from confusion and distress; my kind protector informed me of the cause, said I had some grains of marechale powder in my hair perhaps, and led me out of the assembly, to which no entreaties could prevail on me ever to return, or make further attempts to associate with a delicacy so very susceptible of offence.

Meantime the weather is exceedingly bad—heavy, thick, and foggy as our own, for aught I see; but so it was at Milan, too, I well remember: one's eye would not reach many mornings across the Naviglio that ran directly under our windows. For fine, bright Novembers we must go to Constantinople, I fancy; certain it is that Rome will not supply them.

What, however, can make these Roman ladies fly from *odori* so, that a drop of lavender-water in one's handkerchief, or a carnation in one's stomacher, is to throw them all into convulsions thus? Sure this is the only instance in which they forbear to 'fabbricare su l'antico,'* in their own phrase; the dames, of whom Juvenal delights to tell, liked perfumes well enough, if I remember, and Horace and Martial cry 'Carpe rosas' perpetually. Are the modern inhabitants still more refined than they in their researches

* 'Build upon the old foundations.'

after pleasure? and are the present race of ladies capable of increasing, beyond that of their ancestors, the keenness of any corporeal sense? I should think not. Here are, however, amusements enough at Rome without trying for their conversations.

The Barberini Palace, whither I carried a distracting toothache, amused even that torture by the variety of its wonders.

Nothing can equal the nastiness at one's entrance to this magazine of perfection; but the Roman nobles are not disgusted with all sorts of scents, it is plain. These are not what we should call perfumes, indeed, but certainly *odori*—of the same nature as those one is obliged to wade through before Trajan's Pillar can be climbed.

That the general appearance of a city which contains such treasures should be mean and disgusting, while one literally often walks upon granite and tramples red porphyry under one's feet, is one of the greatest wonders to me in a town of which the wonders seem innumerable; that it should be nasty beyond all telling, all endurance, with such perennial streams of the purest water liberally dispersed and triumphantly scattered all over it, is another unfathomable wonder; that so many poor should be suffered to beg in the streets when not a hand can be got to work in the fields, and that those poor should be permitted to exhibit sights of deformity and degradations of our species, to me unseen till now, at the most solemn moments, and in churches where silver and gold and richly-arrayed priests scarcely suffice to call off attention from their squalid miseries, I do not try to comprehend. That the palaces which taste and expense combine to decorate should look quietly on while common passengers use their noble vestibules, nay stairs, for every nauseous purpose; that princes, whose incomes equal those of our Dukes of Bedford and Marlborough, should suffer their servants to dress other men's dinners for hire, or lend out their equipages for a day's pleasuring, and hang wet rags out of their palace-windows to dry, as at the mean habitation of a pauper, while, looking in at those very windows, nothing is to be seen but proofs of opulence and scenes of splendour, I will not undertake to explain. Sure I am that whoever knows Rome will not condemn this *ébauche* of it.

When I spoke of their beggars, many not unlike Salvator Rosa's 'Job' at the Santa Croce Palace, I ought not to have omitted their eloquence and various talents. We talked to a lame man one day at our own door, whose account of his illness would not have disgraced a medical professor, so judicious were his sentiments, so scientific was his discourse. The accent here, too, is perfectly pleasing, intelligible, and expressive, and I like their *cantilena* vastly.

The excessive lenity of all Italian States makes it dangerous to live among them—a seeming paradox, yet certainly most true; and whatever is evil in this way at any other town is worst at Rome, where those who deserve hanging enjoy almost a moral certainty of never being hanged, so unwilling is everybody to detect the offender, and so numerous the churches to afford him protection if found out.

A man asked importunately in our antechamber this morning for the *padrone*, naming no names, and our servants turned him out. He went, however, only five doors further, found a sick old gentleman sitting in his lodging, attended by a feeble servant, whom he bound, stuck a knife in the master, rifled the apartments, and walked coolly out again at noon-day; nor should we have ever heard of such a trifle, but that it happened just by so, for here are no newspapers to tell who is murdered, and nobody's pity is excited, unless for the malefactor when they hear he is caught.

But the Palazzo Farnese is a more pleasing speculation. There were several broken statues in the place, and while my companions were examining the group after I had done, the wench's conversation who showed it made my amusement. As we looked together at an Egyptian Isis, or, as many call her, the 'Ephesian Diana,' with a hundred breasts, very hideous, and swathed about the legs like a mummy at Cairo, or a baby at Rome, I said, to the girl :

'They worshipped these filthy things formerly, before Jesus Christ came ; but He taught us better,' added I, 'and we are wiser now. How foolish, was not it, to pray to this ugly stone ?'

'The people were wickeder then, very likely,' replied my friend the wench ; 'but I do not see that it was foolish at all.'

Who says the modern Romans are degenerated ? I swear I think them so like their ancestors, that it is my delight to contemplate the resemblance. A statue of a peasant carrying game at this very palace is habited precisely in the modern dress, and shows how very little change has yet been made. The shoes of the low fellows, too, particularly attract my notice ; they exactly resemble the ancient ones.

After three days more we go to Naples—news perfectly agreeable to me, who never have been well here for two hours together. All the great churches remain yet unvisited; they are to be taken at our return in spring.

Vopiscus said that the statues in his time at Rome outnumbered the people, and I trust the remark is now almost doubly true, as every day and hour digs up dead worthies, and the unwholesome weather must surely send many of the living ones to their ancestors. Upon the whole, the men and women of porphyry, etc., please me best, as they do not handle long knives to so good an effect as the others do—'qui aime bien a s'égorger encore,'* says a French gentleman of them the other day. There is, however, an air of cheerfulness in the streets at a night among the poor, who fry fish and eat roots, sausages, etc., as they walk about gaily enough, and though they quarrel too often, never get drunk at least.

* 'Who have still a taste to be cut-throats.'

CHAPTER IX

NAPLES

Eruption of Vesuvius—St. Januarius—Tattooing—Lazaroni—Horses—Character of the People—Masaniello—The King of Naples—A Penitent—Dirty Churches—Murder by a Friar—Dress—The Grotta del Cane—Christmas Festivities—Fatal Accidents—Two Assemblies—A Sicilian Prince—Marriage—Earthquake at Messina—Early Spring—Castle of St. Elmo—The Hermit of Vesuvius—Baiæ—A Masquerade—An Englishman in a Farce—Policinello—Water in the Streets.

ON the tenth day of this month we arrived early at Naples, for I think it was about two o'clock in the morning; and sure the providence of God preserved us, for never was such weather seen by me since I came into the world: thunder, lightning, storm at sea, rain and wind contending for mastery, and combining to extinguish the torches bought to light us the last stage; Vesuvius, vomiting fire, and pouring torrents of red-hot lava down its sides, was the only object visible; and that we saw plainly in the afternoon thirty miles off, where I asked a Franciscan friar if it was the famous volcano. 'Yes,' replied he, 'that's our mountain, which throws up money for us, by calling foreigners to see the extraordinary effects of so surprising a phenomenon.' The weather was quiet then, and we had no notion of passing such a horrible night; but an hour after dark a storm came on, which was really dreadful to endure, or even look upon. The blue lightning, whose colour showed the nature of the original minerals from which she drew her existence, shone round us in a broad expanse from time to time, and sudden darkness followed in an instant; no object then but the fiery river could be seen, till another flash discovered the waves tossing and breaking at a height I never saw before.

Nothing sure was ever more sublime or awful than our entrance into Naples at the dead hour we arrived, when not a whisper was to be heard in the streets, and not a glimpse of light was left to guide us, except the small lamp hung now and then at a high window before a favourite image of the Virgin.

My poor maid had by this time nearly lost her wits with terror, and the French valet, crushed with fatigue, and covered with rain and sea-spray, had just life enough left to exclaim: 'Ah, madame! il me semble que nos sommes venus ici exprès pour voir la fin du monde.'*

* 'Lord, madam! why we came here on purpose sure to see the end of the world.'

Naples

The Ville de Londres inn was full, and could not accommodate our family; but calling up the people of the Crocelle, we obtained a noble apartment, the windows of which look full upon the celebrated bay which washes the wall at our door. Caprea lies opposite the drawing-room or gallery, which is magnificent; and my bed-chamber commands a complete view of the mountain, which I value more, and which called me the first night twenty times away from sleep and supper, though never so in want of both as at that moment surely.

Such were my first impressions of this wonderful metropolis, of which I had been always reading summer descriptions, and had regarded somehow as an Hesperian garden—an earthly paradise, where delicacy and softness subdued every danger, and general sweetness captivated every sense; nor have I any reason yet to say it will not still prove so, for though wet and weary and hungry, we wanted no fire, and found only inconvenience from that they lighted on our arrival. It was the fashion at Florence to struggle for a *terreno*, but here we are all perched up one hundred and forty-two steps from the level of the land or sea; large balconies, apparently well secured, give me every enjoyment of a prospect, which no repetition can render tedious; and here we have agreed to stay till spring, which, I trust, will come out in this country as soon as the new year calls it.

Our eagerness to see sights has been repressed at Naples only by finding everything a sight; one need not stir out to look for wonders sure, while this amazing mountain continues to exhibit such various scenes of sublimity and beauty at exactly the distance one would choose to observe it from—a distance which almost admits examination, and certainly excludes immediate fear. When in the silent night, however, one listens to its groaning, while hollow sighs, as of gigantic sorrow, are often heard distinctly in my apartment, nothing can surpass one's sensations of amazement, except the consciousness that custom will abate their keenness. I have not, however, yet learned to lie quiet, when columns of flame, high as the mountain's self, shoot from its crater into the clear atmosphere with a loud and violent noise; nor shall I ever forget the scene it presented one day to my astonished eyes, while a thick cloud, charged heavily with electric matter, passing over, met the fiery explosion by mere chance, and went off in such a manner as effectually baffles all verbal description, and lasted too short a time for a painter to seize the moment and imitate its very strange effect. Monsieur de Vollaire, however, a native of France, long resident in this city, has obtained, by perpetual observation, a power of representing Vesuvius without that black shadow, which others have thought necessary to increase the contrast, but which greatly takes away all resemblance of its original. Upon reflection, it appears to me that the men most famous at London and Paris for performing tricks with fire have been always Italians in my time, and commonly Neapolitans; no wonder, I should think, Naples would produce prodigious connoisseurs in this way. We have almost perpetual lightning of various colours, according to the soil from whence the vapours are exhaled—sometimes of a pale straw or lemon-colour, often white like artificial flame produced by camphor, but oftenest blue, bright as the rays emitted through the coloured liquors set in the window of a chemist's shop in London—and with such thunder!

'For God's sake, sir,' said I to some of them, 'is there no danger of the ships in the harbour here catching fire? Why, we should all fly up in the air directly if once these flashes should communicate to the room where any of the vessels keep their powder.'

'Gunpowder, madam!' replies the man, amazed; 'why, if St. Peter and St. Paul came here with gunpowder on board, we should soon drive them out again. Don't you know,' added he, 'that every ship discharges her contents at such a place' (naming it), 'and never comes into our port with a grain on board?'

Superstition still keeps her footing in this country, and inspires such veneration for St. Januarius, his name, his blood, his statue, etc., that the Neapolitans, who are famous for blasphemous oaths, and a facility of taking the most sacred words into their mouths on every, and I may say on *no*, occasion, are never heard to repeat his name without pulling off their hat, or making some reverential sign of worship at the moment. And I have seen Italians from other States greatly shocked at the grossness of these their unenlightened neighbours, particularly the half-Indian custom of burning figures upon their skins with gunpowder; these figures large and oddly displayed too, according to the coarse notions of the wearer.

As the weather is exceedingly warm, and there is little need of clothing for comfort, our lazaroni have small care about appearances, and go with a vast deal of their persons uncovered, except by these strange ornaments. The man who rows you about this lovely bay, has perhaps the angel Raphael, or the blessed Virgin Mary, delineated on one brawny sun-burnt leg, the saint of the town upon the other.

His arms represent the Glory, or the seven spirits of God, or some strange things, while a brass medal hangs from his neck, expressive of his favourite martyr, who, they confidently affirm, is so madly venerated by these poor uninstructed mortals, that when the mountain burns, or any great disaster threatens them, they beg of our Saviour to speak to St. Januarius in their behalf, and intreat him not to refuse them his assistance. Now though all this was told me by friends of the Romish persuasion—and told me too with a just horror of the superstitious folly—I think my remarks and inferences were not agreeable to them, when expressing my notion that it was only a relic of the adoration originally paid to Janus in Italy.

As to St. Januarius, there certainly was a martyr of that name at Naples, and to him was transferred much of the veneration originally bestowed on the deity from whom he was probably named. One need not, however, wander round the world with Banks and Solander, or stare so at the accounts given us in Cook's voyages of tattooed Indians, when Naples will show one the effects of a like operation, very, very little better executed, on the broad shoulders of numberless lazaroni; and of this there is no need to examine books for information : he who runs over the Chiaja may read in large characters the gross superstition of the Napolitani, who have no inclination to lose their old classical character for laziness:

> 'Et in otia natam
> Parthenopen ;'

says Ovid. I wonder, however, whether our people would work much, surrounded by similar circumstances; I fancy not. Englishmen, poor fellows! must either work or starve. These folks want for nothing—a house would be an inconvenience to them; they like to sleep out of doors, and it is plain they have small care for clothing, as many who possess decent habiliments enough—I speak of the lazaroni—throw almost all off till some holiday, or time of gala, and sit by the seaside playing at moro with their fingers.

A Florentine nobleman told me once, that he asked one of these fellows to carry his portmanteau for him, and offered him a carline—no small sum, certainly, to a Neapolitan, and rather more in proportion than an English shilling—he had not twenty yards to go with it:

'Are you hungry, master?' cries the fellow.

'No,' replied Count Manucci; 'but what of that?'

'Why, then, no more am I,' was the answer;

'and it is too hot weather to carry burdens;' so turned about upon the other side, and lay still.

This class of people, amounting to a number that terrifies one but to think on—some say sixty thousand souls, and experience confirms no less—give the city an air of gaiety and cheerfulness, that one cannot help honestly rejoicing in. The Strada del Toledo is one continual crowd—nothing can exceed the confusion to a walker; and here are little gigs drawn by one horse, which, without any bit in his mouth, but a string tied round his nose, tears along with inconceivable rapidity a small narrow gilt chair, set between the two wheels, and no spring to it, nor anything else which can add to the weight; and this flying car is a kind of fiacre you pay so much for a drive in, I forget the sum.

Horses are particularly handsome in this town, not so large as at Milan, but very beautiful and spirited: the cream-coloured creatures, such as draw our king's state-coach, are a common breed here, and shine like satin; here are some, too, of a shining silver white, wonderfully elegant, and the ladies upon the Corso exhibit a variety scarcely credible in the colour of their cattle which draw them; but the coaches, harness, trappings, etc., are vastly inferior to the Milanese, whose liveries are often splendid, whereas the four or five ill-dressed strange-looking fellows that disgrace the Neapolitan equipages seem to be valued only for their number, and have very often much the air of Sir John Falstaff's recruits.

Yesterday, however, showed me what I knew not had existed—a skew-ball or piebald ass, eminently well-proportioned, coated like a racer in an English stud, sixteen hands and a half high, his colour bay and white in large patches, and his temper, as the proprietor told me, singularly docile and gentle. I have longed, perhaps, to purchase few things in my life more earnestly than this beautiful and useful animal, which I might have had for two pounds fifteen shillings English, but dared not, lest, like Dogberry, I should have been written down for an ass by my merry country-folks, who, I remember, could not let the Queen of England herself possess in peace a creature of the same kind, but handsomer still, and from a still hotter climate, called the zebra.

Apropos to quadrupeds, when Portia, in the 'Merchant of Venice,' enumerates her lovers, she names the Neapolitan prince first; who, she says, does nothing, for his part, but talk of his horse, and makes it his greatest boast that he can shoe him himself. This is almost literally true of a nobleman here; and they really do not throw their pains away, for it is surprising to see what command they have their cattle in, though bits are scarcely used among them.

The coat armour of Naples consists of an unbridled horse, and by what I can make out of their character, they much resemble him—

> 'Qualis ubi abruptis fugit præsepia vinclis
> Tandem liber equus,' etc. ;*

generous and gay, headstrong and violent in their disposition, easy to turn, but difficult to stop. No authority is respected by them when some strong passion animates them to fury; yet lazily quiet, and unwilling to stir till accident rouses them to terror, or rage urges them forward to incredible exertions of suddenly-bestowed strength. In the eruption of 1779 their fears and superstitions rose to such a height that they seized the French ambassador upon the bridge, tore him almost out of his carriage as he fled from Portici, and was met by them upon the Ponte della Maddalena, where they threatened him with instant death if he did not get out of his carriage, and, prostrating himself before the statue of St. Januarius, which stands there, intreat his protection for the city. All this, however, Mons. le Comte de Clermont D'Amboise did not comprehend a word of,

---

* 'Freed from his keepers thus with broken reins
    The wanton courser prances o'er the plains.'
                                                    DRYDEN.

but taking all the money out of his pocket, threw it down, happily for him, at the feet of the figure, and pacified them at once, gaining time by those means to escape their vengeance.

It was, I think, upon some other occasion that Sir William Hamilton's book relates their unworthy treatment of the venerable archbishop, who refused them the relics with which they had no doubt of saving the menaced town; but every time Vesuvius burns with danger to the city, they scruple not to insult their sovereign as he flies from it, throwing large stones after his chariot, guards, etc., making the insurrection it is sure to occasion more perilous, if possible, than the volcano itself. And last night, when 'la montagna fu cattiva,'* as their expression was, our laquais de place observed that it might possibly be because so many heretics and unbelievers had been up it the day before.

I wished exceedingly to purchase here the genuine account of Masaniello's far-famed sedition and revolt, more dreadful in a certain way than any of the earthquakes which have at different times shaken this hollow-founded country. But my friends here tell me it was suppressed, and burned by the hands of the common executioner, with many chastisements

* When the mountain was in ill-humour.

beside bestowed upon the writer, who tried to escape, but found it more prudent to submit to justice.

Thomas Agnello was the unluckily-adapted name of the mad fisherman who headed the mob on that truly memorable occasion; but it is not an unusual thing here to cut off the first syllable, and by the figure aphæresis alter the appellation entirely. By that device of dropping the 'to,' he has been called Masaniello; and this is one of their methods to render the patois of Naples as unintelligible to us as if we had never seen Italy till now, and one is above all things tormented with their way of pronouncing names. Here are Don and Donna again at this town, as at Milan, however, because the King of Spain, or Ré Cattolico, as these people always call him, has still much influence, and they seem to think nearly as respectfully of him as of their own immediate sovereign, who is, however, greatly beloved among them; and so he ought to be, for he is the representative of them all. He rides and rows, and hunts the wild boar, and catches fish in the bay, and sells it in the market—as dear as he can, too—but gives away the money they pay him for it, and that directly; so that no suspicion of meanness, or of anything worse than a little rough merriment, can be ever attached to his truly honest, open, undesigning character.

Stories of monarchs seldom give me pleasure, who seldom am persuaded to give credit to tales told of persons few people have any access to, and whose behaviour towards those few is circumscribed within the laws of insipid and dull routine; but this prince lives among his subjects with the old Roman idea of a window before his bosom, I believe. They know the worst of him is that he shoots at the birds, dances with the girls, eats macaroni, and helps himself to it with his fingers, and rows against the watermen in the bay, till one of them burst out o'bleeding at the nose last week with his uncourtly efforts to outdo the king, who won the trifling wager by this accident—conquered, laughed, and leaped on shore, amidst the acclamations of the populace, who huzzaed him home to the palace, from whence he sent double the sum he had won to the waterman's wife and children, with other tokens of kindness. Meantime, while he resolves to be happy himself, he is equally determined to make no man miserable.

When the emperor and the grand duke talked to him of their new projects for reformation in the Church, he told them he saw little advantage they brought into their states by these new-fangled notions; that when he was at Florence and Milan the deuce a Neapolitan could he find in either, while his capital was crowded with refugees from thence;

that, in short, they might do their way, but he would do his; that he had not now an enemy in the world, public or private, and that he would not make himself any for the sake of propagating doctrines he did not understand, and would not take the trouble to study; that he should say his prayers as he used to do, and had no doubt of their being heard, while he only begged blessings on his beloved people. So if these wise brothers-in-law would learn of him to enjoy life, instead of shortening it by unnecessary cares, he invited them to see him the next morning play a great match at tennis.

The truth is, the jolly Neapolitans lead a coarse life; but it is an unoppressed one. Never, sure, was there in any town a greater show of abundance: no settled market in any given place, I think, but every third shop full of what the French call so properly 'ammunition de bouche,' while whole boars, kids, and small calves dangle from a sort of neat scaffolding, all with their skins on, and make a pretty appearance. Poulterers hang up their animals in the feathers, too, not lay them on boards plucked, as at London or Venice.

The Strada del Toledo is at least as long as Oxford Road, and straight as Bond Street—very wide too; the houses all of stone, and at least eight stories high. Over the shops live people of fashion,

I am told, but the persons of particularly high quality have their palaces in other parts of the town, which town at last is not a large one, but full as an egg; and Mr. Clarke, the antiquarian, who resides here always, informed me that the late distresses in Calabria had driven many families to Naples this year, beside single wanderers innumerable, which wonderfully increased the daily throng one sees passing and repassing. To hear the lazaroni shout and bawl about the streets night and day one would really fancy one's self in a semi-barbarous nation; and a Milanese officer, who has lived long among them, protested that the manners of the great corresponded in every respect with the idea given of them by the little.

It is, however, observable, and surely very praiseworthy, that if the Italians are not ashamed of their crimes, neither are they ashamed of their contrition. I saw this very morning an odd scene at church, which, though new to me, appeared, perhaps from its frequent repetition, to strike no one but myself.

A lady with a long white dress, and veiled, came in her carriage, which waited for her at the door, with her own arms upon it; and three servants, better dressed than is common here, followed, and put a lighted taper in her hand. En cet étât, as the French say, she moved slowly up the church, looking like Jane Shore in the last act, but not so feeble, and, being arrived at the steps of the high altar, threw herself quite upon her face before it, remaining prostrate there at least five minutes, in the face of the whole congregation, who, equally to my amazement, neither stared nor sneered, neither laughed nor lamented, but minded their own private devotions— no mass was saying—till the lady rose, kissed the steps, and bathed them with her tears, mingled with sobs of no affected or hypocritical penitence, I am sure; retiring afterwards to her own seat, where she waited with others the commencement of the sacred office, having extinguished her candle, and apparently lighted her heart. I felt mine quite penetrated by her behaviour.

Let not this story, however, mislead anyone to think that more general decorum or true devotion can be found in churches of the Romish persuasion than in ours—quite the reverse. This burst of penitential piety was in itself an indecorous thing; but it is the nature and genius of the people not to mind small matters. Dogs are suffered to run about and dirty the churches all the time divine service is performing; while the crying of babies, and the most indecent methods taken by the women to pacify them, give one still juster offence. There is no treading for spittle and nastiness of one sort or another, in all the churches of Italy, whose inhabitants allow the filthiness of Naples, but endeavour to justify the disorders of other cities, though I do believe nothing ever equalled the Chiesa de' Cavalieri at Pisa in any Christian land. Santa Giustina at Padua, the Redentore at Venice, St. Peter's at Rome, and some of the least frequented churches at Milan, are exceptions; they are kept very clean, and do not, by the scandalous neglect of those appointed to keep them, disgrace the beauty of their buildings.

Here has, however, been a dreadful accident, which puts such slight considerations out of one's head. A friar has killed a woman in the church just by the Crocelle inn, for having refused him favours he suspected she had granted to another. No step is taken, though, towards punishing the murderer, because he is 'religioso, e di più cavaliere.' What a miracle that more such outrages are not daily committed in a country where profession of sanctity and real high birth are protections from law and justice! Surely nothing but perfect sobriety and great goodness of disposition can be alleged as a reason why worse is not done every day. I said so to a gentleman just now, who assured me the criminal would not escape very severe castigation, and that perhaps the convent would inflict such severities upon that gentleman as would amply supply the want of activity in the exertion of civil power.

It is a stupid thing not to mention the common dress of the ordinary women here, which ladies likewise adopt if they venture out on foot, desiring not to be known. Two black silk petticoats then serve entirely to conceal their own figure, as when both are tied round their waist, one is suddenly turned up, and as they pull it quick over their heads, a loose trimming of narrow black gauze drops over the face, while a hook and eye fastens all close under the chin, and gives them an air not unlike our country wenches, who throw the gown tail over their heads to protect them from a summer's shower. The holiday dresses, meantime, of the peasants round Naples are very rich and cumbersome. One often sees a great coarse, raw-boned fellow on a Sunday panting for heat under a thick blue velvet coat comically enough; the females in a scarlet cloth petticoat, with a broad gold lace at the bottom; a jacket open before, but charged with heavy ornaments, and the head not unbecomingly dressed with an embroidered handkerchief from Turkey, exactly as one sees them represented here in prints, which they sell dear enough, God knows, and ask, as I am informed by the purchasers, not twice or thrice, but four or five times more than at last they take, as, indeed, for everything one buys here.

One portrait is better, however, than a thousand words when single figures are to be delineated; but of the Grotta del Cane description gives a completer idea than drawing. Both are perhaps nearly unnecessary, indeed, when speaking of a place so often and so accurately described. What surprised me most among the ceremonies of this extraordinary place was that the pent-up vapour shut in an excavation of the rock should, upon opening the door, gradually move forwards à few yards, but not rise up above a foot from the surface, nor, by what I could observe, ever dissipate in air. I think we left it hovering over the favourite spot, when the poor cur's nose had been forcibly held in it for a minute or two; but he took care after his recovery to keep a very judicious distance. Sporting with animal life is always highly offensive; and the fellow's account that his dog was used to the operation, and had already gone through it eight times, that it did him no harm, etc., I considered as words used merely to quiet our impatience of the experiment, which is infinitely more amusing when tried upon a lighted flambeau, extinguishing it most completely in a moment. What connection there is between flame and vitality,

THE GROTTO DEL CANE.
From an Etching by Raphael Morghen.

those who know more of the matter than I do must expound.

The Christmas season here at Naples is very pleasingly observed. The Italians are peculiarly ingenious in adorning their shops, I think, and setting out their wares. Every grocer, fruiterer, etc., now mingles orange and lemon and myrtle leaves among the goods exposed at his door, as we do greens in the churches of England, but with infinitely more taste; and this device produces a very fine effect upon the whole, as one drives along la Strada del Toledo, which all morning looks showy from these decorations, and all evening splendid from the profusion of torches, flambeaux, etc., that shine with less regularity, indeed, but with more lustre and greater appearance of expensive gaiety, than our neat, clean, steady London lamps. Some odd, pretty movable coffee-houses, too, or lemonade shops, set on wheels, and adorned, according to the possessor's taste, with gilding, painting, etc., and covered with ices, orgeats, and other refreshments, as in emulation each of the other, and in a strange variety of shapes and forms, too, exquisitely well-imagined for the most part, help forward the finery of Naples exceedingly. I have counted thirty of these *galante* shops on each side of the street, which, with their necessary illuminations, make a brilliant figure by candlelight, till twelve o'clock, when all the show is over, and everybody put out their lights and quietly lie down to rest. Till that hour, however, few things can exceed the tumultuous merriment of Naples, while *volantes*, or running footmen, dressed like tumblers before a show, precede all carriages of distinction, and endeavour to keep the people from being run over; yet whilst they are listening to Policinello's jokes, or to some such street orator as Dr. Moore describes with equal truth and humour, they often get crushed and killed; yet, as Pope says,

'See some strange comfort every state attend.'

The lazaroni who has his child run over by the coach of a man of quality has a regular claim upon him for no less than twelve carlines (about five shillings English); if it is his wife that meets with the accident, he gets two ducats, live or die; and for the master of the family (house he has none) three is the regular compensation; and no words pass here about trifles. Truth is, human life is lower rated in all parts of Italy than with us; they think nothing of an individual, but see him perish (excepting by the hand of justice) as a cat or dog. A young man fell from our carriage at Milan one evening; he was not a servant of ours, but a friend which, after we were gone home, the coachman had picked up to go with him to the fireworks which were exhibited that night near the Corso. There was a crowd and an *embarras*, and the fellow tumbled off and died upon the spot, and nobody even spoke, or I believe thought about the matter, except one woman, who supposed that he had neglected to cross himself when he got up behind.

There is a work of art peculiar to this city, and attempted in no other, on which surprising sums of money are lavished by many of the inhabitants, who connect or associate to this amusement ideas of piety and devotion. The thing when finished is called a *presepio*, and is composed in honour of this sacred season, after which all is taken to pieces, and arranged after a different manner next year. In many houses a room, in some a whole suite of apartments, in others the terrace upon the house-top, is dedicated to this very uncommon show, consisting of a miniature representation in sycamore wood, properly coloured, of the house at Bethlehem, with the blessed virgin, St. Joseph, and our Saviour in the manger, with attendant angels, etc., as in pictures of the nativity. The figures are about six inches high, and dressed with the most exact propriety. This, however, though the principal thing intended to attract spectators' notice, is kept back, so that sometimes I scarcely saw it at all; while a general and excellent landscape, with figures of men at work, women dressing dinner, a long road in real gravel, with rocks, hills, rivers, cattle, camels, everything that can be imagined, fill the other rooms, so happily disposed, too, for the most part, the light introduced so artfully, the perspective kept so surprisingly! One wonders, and cries out it is certainly but a baby-house at best; yet, managed by people whose heads, naturally turned towards architecture and design, give them power thus to defy a traveller not to feel delighted with the general effect; while if every single figure is not capitally executed and nicely expressed beside, the proprietor is truly miserable, and will cut a new cow, or vary the horse's attitude, against next Christmas, coûte que coûte. And perhaps I should not have said so much about the matter if there had not been shown me within this last week *presepios* which have cost their possessors fifteen hundred or two thousand English pounds; and, rather than relinquish or sell them, many families have gone to ruin. I have wrote the sums down in letters, not figures, for fear of the possibility of a mistake. One of these playthings had the journey of the three kings represented in it, and the presents were all of real gold and silver finely

CHRISTMAS EVE IN ROME: CALABRIAN PEASANTS.
From an Etching by David Allan.

worked; nothing could be better or more livelily finished.

'But, sir,' said I, 'why do you dress up one of the wise men with a turban and crescent, six hundred years before the birth of Mahomet, who first put that mark in the forehead of his followers? The eastern magi were not Turks; this is a breach of costume.' My gentleman paused, and thanked me; said he would inquire if there was nothing heretical in the objection; and if all was right, it should be changed next year without fail.

A young lady here of English parents, just ten years old, asked me very pertinently, 'Why this pretty sight was called a *presepio*?' But said she suddenly, answering herself, 'I suppose it is because it is preceptive.'

Let me now tell about the two assemblies, *o sia conversazioni*, where one goes in search of amusement, as to the rooms of Bath or Tunbridge exactly, only that one of these places is devoted to the *nobiltà;* the other is called *de' buoni amici;* and such is the state of subordination in this country that, though the great people may come among the little ones, and be sure of the grossest adulation, a merchant's wife, shining in diamonds, being obliged to stand up reverentially before the chair of a countess, who does her the honour to speak to her, the poor *amici* are totally excluded from the subscription of the nobles, nor dare even to return the salutation of a superior, should a good-natured person of that rank be tempted, from frequently seeing them at the rooms, to give them a kind nod in the street or elsewhere. All this seems comical enough to us, and I had much ado to look grave while a beautiful and well-educated wife of a rich banker here confessed herself not fit company for an ignorant, mean-looking woman of quality. But though such unintelligible doctrines make one for a moment ashamed both of one's sex and species, that lady's knowledge of various languages, her numerous accomplishments in a thousand methods of passing time away with innocent elegance, and a sort of studied address never observed in Italy before, gave me infinite delight in her society, and daily increased my suspicion that she was a foreigner, till nearer intimacy discovered her a German Lutheran, with a singular head of thick blonde hair, so unlike those I see around me. We grew daily better acquainted, and she showed me—but not indignantly at all—some ladies from the higher assembly sitting among these, very low dressed indeed, a knotting-bag and counters in their lap, to show their contempt of the company; while such as spoke to them stood before their seat, like children before a governess in England, as long as the conversation lasted.

Our Duke and Duchess of Cumberland have made all Naples adore them, though, by going richly dressed, and behaving with infinite courtesy and good-humour, at an assembly or ball given in the lower rooms, as the English comically call them. A young Palermitan prince applauded them for it exceedingly, so I took the liberty to express my wonder. 'Oh,' replied he, 'we are not ignorant how much English manners differ from our own. I have already, though but just eighteen years old, as sovereign of my own state, under the King of both Sicilies, condemned a man to death because he was a rascal; but the law and the people govern in England, I know.' My desire of hearing about Sicily, which we could not contrive to visit, made me happy to cultivate Prince Ventimiglia's acquaintance. He was very studious, very learned of his age, and uncommonly clever; told me of the antiquities his island had to boast with great intelligence and a surprising knowledge of ancient history.

It is wonderfully mortifying to think how little information after all can be obtained of anything new or anything strange, though so far from one's own country. What I picked up most curious and diverting from our conversation was his expression of surprise when at our house one day he read a letter from his mother, telling him that such a lady, naming her, remained still unmarried, and even unbetrothed, though now past ten years old.

'She will,' said I, 'perhaps break through old customs and choose for herself, as she is an orphan and has no one whom she need consult.'

'Impossible, madam!' was the reply.

'But tell me, prince, for information's sake, if such a lady—this girl, for example—should venture to assert the rights of humanity, and make a choice somewhat unusual, what would come of it?'

'Why, nothing in the world would come of it,' answered he. 'The lass would be immediately at liberty again, for no man so circumstanced could be permitted to leave the country alive, you know; nor would her folly benefit his family at all, as her estate would be immediately adjudged to the next heir. No person of inferior rank in our country would, therefore, unless absolutely mad, set his life to hazard for the sake of a frolic, the event of which is so well known beforehand.'

I will mention another talk I had with a Sicilian lady. We met, at the house of the Swedish minister, Monsieur André, uncle to the lamented officer who perished in our sovereign's service in America; and while the rest of the company were entertaining themselves with cards and music, I began laughing in myself at hearing the gentleman and lady who sat next me, called by others Don Raphael and Donna Camilla, because those two names bring Gil Blas into one's head. Their agreeable and interesting conversation, however, soon gave my mind a more serious turn. When discoursing on the liberal premiums now offered by the King of Naples to those who are willing to rebuild and repeople Messina, Donna Camilla politely introduced me to a very sick but pleasing looking lady, who she said was going to return thither, at which she, starting, cried, 'Oh, God forbid, my dear friend!' in an accent that made me think she had already suffered something from the concussions that overwhelmed that city in the year 1783. Her inviting manner, her soft and interesting eyes, whose languid glances seemed to show beauty sunk in sorrow, and spirit oppressed by calamity, engaged my utmost attention, while Don Raphael pressed her to indulge the foreigner's curiosity with some particulars of the distresses she had shared. Her own feelings were all she could relate, she said, and those confusedly.

'You see that girl there?' pointing to a child about seven or eight years old, who stood listening to the harpsichord. 'She escaped! I cannot for my soul guess how, for we were not together at the time.'

'Where were you, madam, at the moment of the fatal accident?'

'Who—me?' and her eyes lighted up with recollected terror. 'I was in the nursery with my maid, employed in taking stains out of some Brussels lace upon a brazier, two babies, neither of them four years old, playing in the room. The eldest boy, dear lad! had just left us, and was in his father's country house. The day grew so dark all on a sudden, and the brazier—oh, Lord Jesus! I felt the brazier slide from me, and saw it run down the long room on its three legs. The maid screamed, and I shut my eyes and knelt at a chair. We thought all over; but my husband came, and, snatching me up, cried, "Run! run!" I know not how nor where, but all amongst falling houses it was; and people shrieked so, and there was such a noise! My poor son! he was fifteen years old; he tried to hold me fast in the crowd. I remember kissing him. "Dear lad! dear lad!" I said. I could speak just then; but the throng at the gate! Oh, that gate! Thousands at once! aye, thousands! thousands at once! and my poor old confessor, too! I knew him; I threw my arms about his aged neck. "Padre mio!" said I; "padre mio!" Down he dropt—a great stone struck his shoulder. I saw it coming, and my boy pulled me. He saved my life, dear, dear lad! But the crash of the gate, the screams of the people, the heat—oh, such a heat! I felt no more on't, though; I saw no more on't. I waked in bed, this girl by me, and her father giving me cordials. We were on shipboard, they told me, coming to Naples, to my brother's house here. And do you think I'll ever go back there again? No, no! That's a cursed place; I lost my son in it. Never, never will I see it more! All my friends try to persuade me; but the sight of it would do my business. If my poor boy were alive, indeed; but he! ah, poor lad! he loved his mother; he held me fast—No, no, I'll never see that place again: God has cursed it now; I am sure He has.'

A narrative so melancholy, so tender, and so true, could not fail of its effect. I ran for refuge to the harpsichord, where a lady was singing divinely. I could not listen, though: her grateful sweetness who told the dismal story, followed me thither; she had seen my ill-suppressed tears, and followed to embrace me. The tale she had told saddened my heart, and the news we heard returning to the Crocelle did not contribute to lighten its weight, while an amiable young Englishman, who had long lain ill there, was now breathing his last, far from his friends, his country, or their customs; all easily dispensed with, perhaps derided, during the bustle of a journey, and in the madness of superfluous health; but sure to be sighed after when life's last twilight shuts in precipitately closer and closer round a man, and leaves him only the nearer objects to repose and dwell on.

Such was Captain ——'s situation! he had none but a foreign servant with him. We thought it might soothe him to hear 'Can I do anything for you, sir?' in an English voice, so I sent my maid. He had no commands, he said; he could not eat the jelly she had made him. He wished some clergyman could be found that he might speak to. Such a one was vainly inquired for, till it was discovered that ill-health had driven Mr. Mentze to Naples, who kindly administered the last consolation a Christian can receive; and heard the next day, when confined himself to bed, of his countryman's being properly thrust by the banker into the 'Buco Protestante.' So they contemptuously call a dirty garden one drives by in this town, where not less than a hundred people, small and great, from our island, annually resort, leaving fifty or sixty thousand pounds behind them at a moderate computation; though if their bodies are obliged to take perpetual apartments here, no better place has been hitherto provided for them than this kitchen ground; on which grow cabbages, cauliflowers, etc., sold to their country folks for double price, I trow, the remaining part of the season.

20th January, 1786.

Here are the most excellent, the most incomparable fish I ever eat; red mullets, large as our maycril, and of singularly high flavour; besides the calamaro, or ink-fish, a dainty worthy of imperial luxury; almond and even apple-trees in blossom, to delight those who can be paid for coarse manners and confined notions by the beauties of a brilliant climate. Here are all the hedges in blow as you drive towards Pozzuoli, and a snow of white Mayflowers clustering round Virgil's tomb. So strong was the sun's heat this morning, even before eleven o'clock, that I carried an umbrella to defend me from his rays, as we sauntered about the walks, which are spacious and elegant, laid out much in the style of St. James's Park, but with the sea on one side of you, the broad street, called Chiaja, on the other. What trees are planted there, however, either do not grow up so as to afford shade, or else they cut them, and trim them about to make them in pretty shapes forsooth, as we did in England half a century ago.

The castle on this hill, called the Castel St. Elmo, would be much my comfort did I fix at Naples; for here are eight thousand soldiers constantly kept, to secure the city from sudden insurrection; his majesty most wisely trusting their command only to Spanish or German officers, or some few gentlemen from the northern states of Italy, that no personal tenderness for any in the town below may intervene, if occasion for sudden severity should arise. We went to-day and saw their garrison, comfortably and even elegantly kept; and I was wicked enough to rejoice that the soldiers were never, but with the very utmost difficulty, permitted to go among the townsmen for a moment.

To-morrow we mount the volcano, whose present peaceful disposition has tempted us to inspect it more nearly. Though it appears little less than presumption thus to profane with eyes of examination the favourite alembic of nature, while the great work of projection is carrying on; guarded as all its secret caverns are, too, with every contradiction: snow and flame! solid bodies heated into liquefaction, and rolling gently down one of its sides, while fluids congeal and harden into ice on the other; nothing can exceed the curiosity of its appearance now the lava is less rapid, and stiffens as it flows; stiffens, too, in ridges very surprisingly, and gains an odd aspect, not unlike the pasteboard waves representing sea at a theatre, but black, because this year's eruption has been mingled with coal. The connoisseurs here know the different degrees, dates, and shades of lava to a perfection that amazes one: and Sir William Hamilton's courage, learning, and perfect skill in these matters, is more people's theme here than the volcano itself. Bartolomeo, the Cyclops of Vesuvius as he is called, studies its effects and operations too with much attention and philosophical exactness, relating the adventures he has had with our minister on the mountain to every Englishman that goes up, with great success. The way one climbs is by tying a broad sash with long ends round this Bartolomeo, letting him walk before one, and holding it fast. As far as the hermitage there is no great difficulty, and to that place some choose to ride an ass, but I thought walking safer; and there you are sure of welcome and refreshment from the poor, good old man, who sets up a little cross wherever the fire has stopped near his cell; shows you the place with a sort of polite solemnity that impresses, spreads his scanty provisions before you kindly, and tells the past and present state of the eruption accurately, inviting you to partake of

> 'His rushy couch, his frugal fare,
> His blessing and repose.'
>   GOLDSMITH.

This hermit is a Frenchman. 'J'ai dansé dans

mon lit tant de fois,' said he. The expression was not sublime when speaking of an earthquake, to be sure; I looked among his books, however, and found Bruyère.

'Would not the Duc de Rochefoucault have done better?' said I.

'Did I never see you before, madam?' said he; 'yes, sure I have, and dressed you, too, when I was a hairdresser in London, and lived with Monsieur Martinant. And I dressed pretty Miss Wynne, too, in the same street. Vit-elle encore? Vit-elle encore? Ah, I am old now,' continued he; 'I remember when black pins first came up.'

That the situation of the crater changed in this last eruption is of little consequence; it will change and change again I suppose. The wonder is that nobody gets killed by venturing so near, while red-hot stones are flying about them so. The Bishop of Derry did very near get his arm broke; and the Italians are always recounting the exploits of these rash Britons who look into the crater, and carry their wives and children up to the top; while we are, with equal justice, amazed at the courageous Neapolitans, who build little snug villages and dwell with as much confidence at the foot of Vesuvius, as our people do in Paddington or Hornsey. When I inquired of an inhabitant of these houses how she managed, and whether she was not frightened when the volcano raged, lest it should carry away her pretty little habitation:

'Let it go,' said shè, 'we don't mind now if it goes to-morrow, so as we can make it answer by raising our vines, oranges, etc., against it for three years, our fortune is made before the fourth arrives; and then if the red river comes we can always run away, *scappar via*, ourselves, and hang the property. We only desire three years' use of the mountain as a hot wall or forcing-house, and then we are above the world, thanks be to God and St. Januarius.'

These dear people at Rome and Naples do live so in the very hulk of shipwrecked, or rather foundered Paganism, have their habitation so at the very bottom of the cask, can it fail to retain the scent when the lees are scarce yet dried up, clean or evaporated? That an odd jumble of past and present days, past and present ideas of dignity, events, and even manner of portioning out their time, still confuse their heads, may be observed in every conversation with them; and when a few weeks ago we re-visited, in company of some newly-arrived English friends, the old baths of Baiæ, Locrine lake, etc., Tobias, who rowed us over, bid us observe the Appian Way under the water, where indeed it appears quite clearly, even to the tracks of wheels on its old pavement, made of very large stones; and, seeing me perhaps particularly attentive :

'Yes, madam,' said he, 'I do assure you, that Don Horace and Don Virgil, of whom we hear such a deal, used to come from Rome to their country-seats here in a day, over this very road, which is now overflowed as you see it, by repeated earthquakes, but which was then so good and so unbroken, that if they rose early in the morning they could easily gallop hither against the Ave Maria.'

It was very observable in our second visit paid to the Stuffe San Germano, that they had increased prodigiously in heat since Mount Vesuvius had ceased throwing out fire, though at least fourteen miles from it, and a vast portion of the sea between them. It vexed me to have no thermometer again, but by what one's immediate feelings could inform us, there were many degrees of difference. I could not now bear my hand on any part of them for a moment. The same luckless dog was again produced, and again restored to life—like the lady in Dryden's fables, who is condemned to be hunted, killed, recovered, and set on foot again for the amusement of her tormentors; a story borrowed from the Italian.

Solfaterra burned my fingers as I plucked an incrustation off, which allured me by the beauty of

its colours, and roared with more violence than when I was there before. This horrible volcano is by no means extinguished yet, but seems pregnant with wonders, principally combustible, and likely to break with one at every step: all the earth round it being hollow as a drum, and I should think of no great thickness neither; so plainly does one hear the sighings underneath, which some of the country people imagine to be tortured spirits howling with agony.

It is supposed that Lake Agnano, where the dog is flung in, if the dewy grass do not suffice to recover him with its humidity and freshness, as it often does, is but another crater of another volcano, long ago self-destroyed by scorpion-like suicide; and it is like enough it may be so. There are not wanting, however, those that think, or say at least, how a subterraneous or subaqueous city remains even now under that lake, but lies too deep for inspection.

Though surrounded by such terrifying objects, the Neapolitans are not, I think, disposed to cowardly, though easily persuaded to devotional superstitions; they are not afraid of spectres or supernatural apparitions, but sleep contentedly and soundly in small rooms, made for the ancient dead, and now actually in the occupation of old Roman bodies—the catacombs belonging to whom are still very impressive to the fancy; and I have known many an

English gentleman, who would not endure to have his courage impeached by living wight, whose imagination would, notwithstanding, have disturbed his slumbers not a little, had he been obliged to pass one night where these poor women sleep securely, wishing only for that money which travellers are not unwilling to bestow; and perhaps a walk among these hollow caves of death, these sad repositories of what was once animated by valour and illuminated by science, strikes one much more than all the urns and lachrymatories of Portici.

The Queen of Naples is delivered, and we are all to make merry; the Castello d' Uovo, just under our windows, is to be illuminated; and from the Carthusian convent on the hill, to my poor solitary old acquaintance the hermit and hair-dresser who inhabits a cleft in Mount Vesuvius, all resolve to be happy, and to rejoice in the felicity of a prince that loves them. Shouting, and candles, and torches, and coloured lamps, and Policinello above all the rest, did their best to drive forward the general joy, and make known the birth of the royal baby for many miles round the capital; and there was a splendid opera the next night, in this finest of all fine theatres, though that of Milan pleases me better; as I prefer the elegant curtains which festoon it over the boxes there, to our heavy gilt ornaments here at Naples; and their boasted looking-glasses, never cleaned, have no effect, as I perceive, towards helping forward the enchantment. A festa di ballo, or masquerade, given here, however, was exceedingly gay, and the dresses surprisingly rich: our party, a very large one, all Italians, retired at one in the morning to quite the finest supper of its size I ever saw. Fish of various sorts, incomparable in their kinds, composed eight dishes of the first course; we had thirty-eight set on the table in that course, forty-nine in the second, with wines and dessert truly magnificent—for all which Mr. Piozzi protested to me that we paid only three shillings and sixpence a head English money; but for the truth of that he must answer. We sat down twenty-two persons to supper, and I observed there were numbers of these parties made in different taverns, or apartments adjoining to the theatre, whither, after refreshment, we returned and danced till daylight.

The theatre is a vast building, even when not inhabited or set off by lights and company; all of stone too, like that of Milan; but particularly defended from fire by St. Anthony, who has an altar and chapel erected to his honour, and showily decorated at the door; and on Sunday night, January 22nd, there were fireworks exhibited in honour of himself and his pig, which was placed on the top, and illuminated with no small ingenuity: the fire catching hold of his tail first—con rispetto—as said our cicerone. But 'Il Rè Lear e le sue tre Figlie' is advertised, and I am sick to-night and cannot go.

My loss, however, is somewhat compensated; for though I could not see our own Shakespeare's play acted at Naples, I went some days after to one of the charming theatres this town is entertained by every evening, and saw a play which struck me exceedingly. The plot was simply this: an Englishman appears, dressed precisely as a Quaker, his hat on his head, his hands in his pockets, and with a very pensive air says he will take that pistol, producing one, and shoot himself; 'for,' says he, 'the politics go wrong at home now, and I hate the ministerial party, so England does not please me. I tried France, but the people there laughed so about nothing, and sung so much out of tune, I could not bear France; so I went over to Holland. Those Dutch dogs are so covetous and hard-hearted, they think of nothing but their money; I could not endure a place where one heard no sound in the whole country but frogs croaking and ducats chinking. Maladetti! so I went to Spain, where I narrowly escaped a sun-stroke for the sake of seeing those idle beggarly dons, that if they do condescend to cobble a man's shoe, think they must do it with a sword by their side. I came here to Naples, therefore, and though it is so fine a country, one can get no fox-hunting, only running after a wild pig. Yes, yes; I must shoot myself; the world is so very dull I'm tired on't.'

He then coolly prepares matters for the operation, when a young woman bursts into his apartment, bewails her fate for a moment, and then faints away. Our countryman lays by his pistol, brings the lady to life, and having heard part of her story, sets her in a place of safety. More confusion follows; a gentleman enters, storming with rage at a treacherous friend he hints at, and a false mistress; the Englishman gravely advises him to shoot himself:

'No, no,' replies the warm Italian; 'I will shoot them though, if I can catch them; but want of money hinders me from prosecuting the search.'

That, however, is now instantly supplied by the generous Briton, who enters into their affairs, detects and punishes the rogue who had betrayed them all, settles the marriage and reconciliation of his new friends, adds himself something to the good girl's fortune, and concludes the piece with saying that he has altered his intentions, and will think no more of shooting himself, while life may in all countries be rendered pleasant to him who will employ it in the service of his fellow-creatures; and finishes with these words, that 'Such are the sentiments of an Englishman.'

But I am called from my observations and reflections, to see what the Neapolitans call 'Il trionfo di Policinello,' a person for whom they profess peculiar value. Harlequin and Brighella here scarcely share the fondness of an audience, while at Venice, Milan, etc., much pleasantry is always cast into their characters.

The triumph was a pageant of prodigious size, set on four broad wheels like our waggons, but larger; it consisted of a pyramid of men, twenty-eight in number, placed with wonderful ingenuity all of one size, something like what one has seen exhibited at Sadler's Wells, the Royal Circus, etc.; dressed in one uniform, viz., the white habit and puce-coloured mask of caro Policinello; disposed too with that skill which tumblers alone can either display or describe; a single figure, still in the same dress, crowning the whole, and forming a point at the top, by standing fixed on the shoulders of his companions, and playing merrily on the fiddle; while twelve oxen of a beautiful white colour, and trapped with many shining ornaments, drew the whole slowly over the city, amidst the acclamations of innumerable spec-

A NEAPOLITAN DANCE.

From an Etching by David Allan.

tators, that followed and applauded the performance with shouts.

What I have learned from this show, and many others of the same kind, is of no greater value than the derivation of his name who is so much the favourite of Naples: but from the mask he appears in, cut and coloured so as exactly to resemble a flea, with hook nose and wrinkles, like the body of that animal; his employment, too, being ever ready to hop, and skip, and jump about, with affectation of uncommon elasticity, giving his neighbours a sly pinch from time to time: all these circumstances, added to the very intimate acquaintance and connection all the Neapolitans have with this, the least offensive of all the innumerable insects that infest them; and, last of all, his name, which, corrupt it how we please, was originally Pulicinello; leaves me persuaded that the appellation is merely 'little flea.'

Van Vittelli's aqueduct is a prodigiously beautiful, magnificent, and what is more, a useful performance. Having the finest models of antiquity, he is said to have surpassed them all. Why such superb and expensive methods should be still used to conduct water up and down Italy, any more than other nations, or why they are not equally necessary in France and England, nobody informs me. Madame de Bocages inquired long ago, when she was taken to see the fountain Trevi at Rome, why they had no water at Paris but the Seine? I think the question so natural, that one wishes to repeat it; and one great reason, little urged by others, incites me to look with envy on the delicious and almost innumerable gushes of water that cool the air of Naples and of Rome, and pour their pellucid tides through almost every street of those luxurious cities: it is this, that I consider them as a preservative against that dreadfullest of all maladies, canine madness—a distemper which, notwithstanding the excessive heat, has here scarcely a name. Sure it is the plenty of drink the dogs meet at every turn, that must be the sole cause of a blessing so desirable.

My stay has always been much shorter than I wished it, in every great town of Italy; but here! where numberless wonders strike the sense without fatiguing it, I do feel double pleasure; and among all the new ideas I have acquired since England lessened to my sight upon the sea, those gained at Naples will be the last to quit me.

Everyone who leaves her carries off the same sensations. I have asked several inhabitants of other Italian States what they liked best in Italy except home; it was Naples always, dear delightful Naples!

CHAPTER X

ROME REVISITED

The Carnival—Pius VI.—The Fireworks—Early Marriages—Villa Albani—A Deaf and Dumb School—Decline of Convents—Spring—Cheap Living.

WE are come here just in time to see the three last days of the carnival, and very droll it is to walk or drive, and see the people run about the streets, all in some gay disguise or other, and masked, and patched, and painted to make sport. The Corso is now quite a scene of distraction; the coachmen on the boxes pretending to be drunk, and throwing sugar-plums at the women, which it grows hard to find out in the crowd and confusion, as the evening, which shuts in early, is the festive hour: and there is some little hazard in parading the streets, lest an accident might happen; though a temporary rail and trottoir are erected, to keep the carriages off. Our high joke, however, seems to consist in the men putting on girls' clothes. A woman is somewhat a rarity at Rome, and strangely superfluous as it should appear by the extraordinary substitutes found for them on the stage: it is more than wonderful to see great strong fellows dancing the women's parts in these fashionable dramas, pastoral and heroic ballets as they call them. Soprano singers did not so surprise me with their feminine appearance in the opera; but these clumsy figurantes! all stout, coarse-looking men, kicking about in hooped petticoats, were to me irresistibly ridiculous; the gentlemen with me, however, both Italians and English, were too much disgusted to laugh, while la première danseuse acted the coquette beauty, or distracted mother, with a black beard which no art could subdue, and destroyed every illusion of the pantomime at a glance. All this struck nobody but us foreigners after all: tumultuous, and often tender applauses from the pit convinced us of their heartfelt approbation! and in the parterre sat gentlemen much celebrated at Rome for their taste and refinement.

As their exhibition did not please our party, notwithstanding its singularity, we went but once to the theatre, except when a Festa di Ballo was advertised to begin at eleven o'clock one night, but detained the company waiting on its stairs for two hours at least beyond the time. For my own part, I was better amused outside the doors than in. Mas-

ROME: A FETE ON THE PIAZZA NAVONA.

From an Engraving by Vasi.

querades can of themselves give very little pleasure except when they are new things. What was most my delight and wonder to observe, was the sight of perhaps two hundred people of different ranks, all in my mind strangely ill-treated by a nobleman; who, having a private supper in the room, prevented their entrance who paid for admission; all mortified, all crowded together in an inconvenient place; all suffering much from heat, and more from disappointment; yet all in perfect good humour with each other, and with the gentleman who detained in longing and ardent, but not impatiently-expressed expectation, such a number of Romans, who, as I could not avoid remarking, certainly deserve to rule over all the world once more, if, as we often read in history, command is to be best learned from the practice of obedience.

The masquerade was carried on, when we had once begun it, with more taste and elegance here than either at Naples or Milan; so it was at Florence, I remember; more dresses of contrivance and fancy being produced. We had a very pretty device last night, of a man who pretended to carry statues about as if for sale; the gentlemen and ladies who personated the figures were incomparable from the choice of attitudes, and skill in colouring; but 'il carnovale è morto,' as the women of quality told us last night from their coaches, in which they carried little transparent lanterns of a round form, red, blue, green, etc., to help forward the shine; and these they throw at each other as they did sugar-plums in the other towns, while the millions of small, thin bougie candles held in every hand, and stuck up at every balcony, make the Strada del Popolo as light as day, and produce a wonderfully pretty effect, gay, natural and pleasing.

The unstudied hilarity of Italians is very rejoicing to the heart, from one's consciousness that it is the result of cheerfulness really felt, not a mere incentive to happiness hoped for. The death of Carnovale, who was carried to his grave with so many candles suddenly extinguished at twelve o'clock last night, has restored us to a tranquil possession of ourselves, and to an opportunity of examining the beauties of nature and art that surround one. . . .

Nothing can look very grand in St. Peter's church; and though I saw the general benediction given (I hope partook it) upon Easter Day, my constant impression was, that the people were below the place; no pomp, no glare, no dove and glory on the chair of state, but what looked too little for the area that contained them. Sublimity disdains to catch the vulgar eye, she elevates the soul; nor can long-drawn processions, or splendid ceremonies, suffice to content those travellers who seek for images that never tarnish, and for truths that never can decay. Pius Sextus, in his morning dress, paying his private devotions at the altar, without any pageantry, and with very few attendants, struck me more a thousand and a thousand times, than when arrayed in gold, in colours, and diamonds, he was carried to the front of a balcony big enough to have contained the conclave; and there, shaded by two white fans, which, though really enormous, looked no larger than that a girl carries in her pocket, pronounced words which, on account of the height they came from, were difficult to hear.

All this is known and felt by the managers of these theatrical exhibitions so certainly, that they judiciously confine great part of them to the Capella Sistina, which, being large enough to impress the mind with its solemnity, and not spacious enough for the priests, congregation, and all, to be lost in it, is well adapted for those various functions that really make Rome a scene of perpetual gala during the Holy Week—which an English friend here protested to me he had never spent with so little devotion in his life before. The 'Miserere' has, however, a strong power over one's mind—the absence of all instrumental music, the steadiness of so many human voices, the gloom of the place, the picture of Michael Angelo's 'Last Judgment' covering its walls, united with the mourning dress of the spectators—is altogether calculated, with great ingenuity, to give a sudden stroke to the imagination, and kindle that temporary blaze of devotion it is wisely enough intended to excite. But even this has much of its effect destroyed, from the admission of too many people; crowd and bustle, and struggle for places, leave no room for any ideas to range themselves, and least of all, serious ones; nor would the opening of our sacred music in Westminster Abbey, when nine hundred performers join to celebrate Messiah's praises, make that impression which it does upon the mind, were not the king, and court, and all the audience as still as death, when the first note is taken.

The ceremony of washing the pilgrims' feet is a pleasing one. It is seen in high perfection here at Rome, where all that the Pope personally performs is done with infinite grace, and with an air of mingled majesty and sweetness, difficult to hit, but singularly becoming in him who is both priest of God and sovereign of his people.

'But how,' said Cyrus, 'shall I make men think me more excellent than themselves?' 'By being really so,' replies Xenophon, putting his words into the mouth of Cambyses. Pius Sextus takes no deeper method, I believe, yet all acknowledge his superior merit. No prince can less affect state, nor no clergyman can less adopt hypocritical behaviour. The Pope powders his hair like any other of the Cardinals, and is, it seems, the first who has ever done so. When he takes the air it is in a fashionable carriage, with a few, a very few guards on horseback, and is by no means desirous of making himself a show. Now and then an old woman begs his blessing as he passes; but I almost remember the time when our bishops of Bangor and St. Asaph were followed by the country people in North Wales full as much or more, and with just the same feelings. One man in particular we used to talk of, who came from a distant part of our mountainous province, with much expense in proportion to his abilities, poor fellow, and terrible fatigue; he was a tenant of my father's, who asked him how he ventured to undertake so troublesome a journey. 'It was to get my good lord's blessing,' replied the farmer; 'I hope it will cure my rheumatism.' Kissing the slipper at Rome will probably, in a hundred years more, be a thing to be thus faintly recollected by a few very old people; and it is strange to me it should have lasted so long. No man better knows than the present learned and pious successor of St.

Peter, that St. Peter himself would permit no act of adoration to his own person; and that he severely reproved Cornelius for kneeling to him, charging him to rise and stand upon his feet, adding these remarkable words, 'Seeing I also am a man.'* Surely it will at last be found out among them that such a ceremony is inconsistent with the Pope's character as a Christian priest, however it may suit state matters to continue it in the character of a sovereign. The roads he is now making on every side his capital to facilitate foreigners' approach, the money he has laid out on the conveniences of the Vatican, the desire he feels of reforming a police much in want of reformation, joined to an immaculate character for private virtue and an elegant taste for the fine arts, must make every one wish for a long continuance of his health and dignity; though the wits and jokers, when they see his arms up, as they are often placed in galleries, etc., about the palace, and consist of a zephyr blowing on a flower, a pair of eagle's wings, and a few stars—have invented this epigram, to say that when the Emperor has got his eagle back, the king of France his fleurs-de-lys, and the stars are gone to heaven, Braschi will have nothing left him but the wind:

> 'Redde aquilam Cæsari, Francorum lilia regi,
> Sidera redde polo, cœtera Brasche tibi.'

---

* 'Surge, et ego ipse homo sum.'—VULGATE.

The Pontine Marshes: the Pope and the Papal Guards.
From an Etching by Raphael Morghen.

These verses were given me by an agreeable Benedictine friar, member of a convent belonging to St. Paul's *fuor delle mura;* he was a learned man, a native of Ragusa, had been particularly intimate with Wortley Montagu, whose variety of acquirements had impressed him exceedingly.

He showed us the curiosities of his church, the finest in Rome next to St. Peter's, and had silver gates—but the plating is worn off and only the brass remains. There is an old Egyptian candlestick above five feet high preserved here, and many other singularities adorn the church. Here is an altar supported by four pillars of red porphyry, and here are the pictures of all the popes; St. Peter first, and our present Braschi last. It has given much occasion for chat that there should now be no room left to hang a successor's portrait, and that he who now occupies the chair is painted in powdered hair and a white head-dress, such as he wears every day, to the great affliction of his courtiers, who recommended the usual state diadem, but 'No, no,' said he, 'there have been red cap Popes enough, mine shall be only white'—and white it is.

This beautiful edifice was built by the Emperor Theodosius, and there is an old picture at the top, of our Saviour giving the benediction in the form that all the Greek priests give it now. Apropos, there have been many sects of Oriental Christians dropped into the Church of Rome within these later years; a very venerable old Armenian says Greek mass regularly in St. Peter's church every day before one particular altar; his long black dress and white beard attracted much of my notice—he saw it did, and now whenever we meet in the street by chance he kindly stands still to bless me. But the Syriac, or Maronites, have a church to themselves just by the Bocca della Verita; and extremely curious we thought it to see their ceremonies upon Palm Sunday, when their aged patriarch, not less than ninety-three years old, and richly attired with an inconvenient weight of drapery, and a mitre shaped like that of Aaron in our Bibles exactly, was supported by two olive-coloured orientals, while he pronounced a benediction on the tree that stood near the altar, and was at least ten feet high. The attendant clergy, habited after their own Eastern taste, and very superbly, had broad phylacteries bound on their foreheads after the fashion of the Jews, and carried long strips of parchment up and down the church, with the law written on them in Syriac characters, while they formed themselves into a procession and led their truly reverend principal back to his place. An exhibition so striking, with the view of many monuments round the walls, sacred to the memory of such and such a bishop of Damascus, gave so strong an impression of Asiatic manners to the mind, that one felt glad to find Europe round one at going out again.

The fireworks exhibited on the castle of St. Angelo on Easter-Day are the completest things of their kind in the world; three thousand rockets all sent up into the air at once, make a wonderful burst indeed, and serve as a pretty imitation of Vesuvius. The lighting up of the building, too, on a sudden with fire-pots, had a new and beautiful effect; we all liked the entertainment vastly.

The *vecchia* is here at Rome the common phrase when speaking of your only female servant, a person not unlike an Oxford or Cambridge bed-maker in appearance; and much amazed was I two days ago at the answer of our *vecchia*, when curiosity prompted me to ask her age:

'Oh, madam, I am a very aged woman,' was the reply, 'and have two grandchildren married; I am forty-two years old, poveretta me!'

I told an Italian gentleman who dined with us what Caterina had said, and begged him to ask the laquais de place, who waited on us at table, a similar question. He appeared a large, well-looking, sturdy fellow, about thirty-eight years old—but said he was scarce twenty-two; that he had been married six years and had five children.

'How old was your wife when you met?'

'Thirteen, sir,' answered Carlo.

So all is kept even at least; for if they end life sooner than in colder climates, they begin it earlier, it is plain.

Yet such things seem strange to us; so do a thousand which occur in these warm countries in the commonest life. Brick floors, for example, with hangings of a dirty, printed cotton, affording no bad shelter for spiders, bugs, etc.; a table in the same room, encrusted with *verd antique*, very fine and worthy of Wilton house; with some exceeding good copies of the finest pictures here at Rome; form the furniture of our present lodging; and now we have got the little casement windows clean to look at it, I pass whole hours admiring, even in the copy, our glorious descent from the cross, by Daniel di Volterra.

Pius Sextus has had a legacy left him within these last years, to the prejudice of some nobleman's heirs; who loudly lamented their fate, and his tyranny who could take advantage, as they expressed it, of their relation's caprice. The Pope did not give it them back, because they behaved so ill, he said; but neither did he seize what was left him by dint of despotic authority; he went to law with the family for it, which I thought a very strange thing; and lost his cause, which I thought a still stranger.

Villa Albani is the most dazzling of any place yet; and the caryatid pillars the finest things in it, though replete with wonders, and distracting with objects each worthy a whole day's attention. Here is an antique list of Euripides' plays in marble, as those tell me who can read the Greek inscriptions; I lose infinite pleasure every day, for want of deeper learning.

What has most struck me here as a real improvement upon social and civil life, was the school of Abate Sylvester, who, upon the plan of Monsieur L'Epée at Paris, teaches the deaf and dumb people to speak, read, write, and cast accounts; he likewise teaches them the principles of logic, and instructs them in the sacred mysteries of our holy religion. I am not naturally credulous, nor apt to take payment in words for meanings; much of my life has been spent, and all my youth, in the tuition of babies; I was of course less likely to be deceived; and I can safely say that they did appear to have learned all he taught them. That appearance, too, if it were no more, is so difficult to obtain, the patience required from the master is so very great, and the good he is doing to mankind so extensive, that I did not like offensively to detect the difference between knowing a syllogism and appearing to know it. With regard to morality, the pupils have certainly gained many præcognita. While the capital scholars were showing off to another party, I addressed a girl who sat working in the window, and perceived that she could explain the meaning of the commandments competently well. To prove the truth, I pretended to pick a gentleman's pocket who stood near me. 'Peccato!' said the wench distinctly—she was about ten years old perhaps; but a little boy of seven was deservedly the master's favourite; he really possessed the most intelligent and interesting countenance I ever saw, and when to explain the major, minor and consequence, he put the two first together into his hat with an air of triumph, we were enchanted with him. Someone, to tease him, said he had red hair; he instantly led them to a picture of our Saviour, which hung in the room, said it was the same colour as His, and ought to be respected.

The Italians seem to find out, I know not why, that it is a good thing the Jesuits are gone; though

A HERMIT ON THE APPIAN WAY.

From an Etching by David Allan.

they steadily endeavour to retain those principles of despotism which it was their peculiar province to inspire and confirm, and whilst all men must see that the work of education goes on worse in other hands. Indeed, nothing can be wilder than committing youth to the tuition of monks and nuns, unless, like them, they were intended for the cloister.

We have been led to reflections of this sort by a view of girls portioned here at Rome once a year, some for marriage, and others for a nunnery; the last set were handsomest and fewest, and the people I converse with say that every day makes an almost visible diminution in the number of monks and nuns. I know not, however, whether Italy will go on much the better for having so few convents; some should surely be left, nay some must be left in a country where it is not possible for every man to obtain a decent livelihood by labour, as in England; no army, no navy, very little commerce possible to the inland states, and very little need of it in any; little study of the law, too, where the prince or baron's lips pronounce on the decision of property. What must people do where so few professions are open? Can they all be physicians, priests, or shopkeepers, where little physic is taken, and few goods bought? There are already more clergy than can live, and I saw an *abate* with the *petit collet* at Lucca, playing in the orchestra at the opera for eighteenpence pay.

And now with regard to the present state of morals at Rome, one must not judge from staring stories told one; it is like Heliogabalus's method of computing the number of his citizens from the weight of their cobwebs. It is wonderful to me the people are no worse, where no methods are taken to keep them from being bad.

As to the society, I speak not from myself, for I saw nothing of it; some English liked it, but more complained. Wanting amusement, however, can be no complaint, even without society, in a city so pregnant with wonders, so productive of reflections; and if the Roman nobles are haughty, who can wonder—when one sees doors of agate, and chimney-pieces of amethyst, one can scarcely be surprised at the possessors' pride, should they in contempt turn their backs upon a foreigner, whom they are early taught to consider as the Turks consider women—creatures formed for their use only, or at best amusement, and devoted to certain destruction at the hour of death. With such principles, the hatred and scorn they naturally feel for a Protestant will easily swell into superciliousness, or burst out into arrogance, the moment it is unrestrained by the necessity of forms among the rich, and the desire of pillage in the poor.

But I shall be glad now to exchange lapis lazuli for violets, and verd antique for green fields. Here are more amethysts about Rome than lilacs; and the laburnum which at this gay season adorns the environs of London, I look for in vain about the Porta del Popolo. The proud purple tulip which decorates the ground hereabouts opposed to the British harebell, is Italy and England again; but the harebell by cultivation becomes a hyacinth, the tulip remains where it began. We are now at the 16th of April, yet I know not how or why it is, although the oaks, young, small, and straggling as they are, have the leaves come out all broad and full already, though the fig is bursting out every day and hour, and the mulberry tree, so tardy in our climate, that I have often been unable to see scarcely a bud upon them even in May, is here completely furnished, apple trees are yet in blossom round this city, and the few elms that can be found are but just unfolding. Common shrubs continue their wintry appearance, and in the general look of spring little is gained. The hedges, now, of Kent and Surrey are filled with fragrance I am sure, and primroses in the remoter provinces torment the sportsmen with spoiling the drag on a soft scenting morning; while limes, horse-chestnuts, etc., contribute to produce an effect not so inferior to that fostered by Italian sunshine, as I expected to find it.

Why the first breath of far-distant summer should thus affect the oak and fig, yet leave the elm and apple as with us, the botanists must tell; few advances have been made in vegetation since we left Naples, that is certain—the hedges were as forward near Pozzuoli two full months ago. And here are no China oranges to be bought; no, nor a cherry or strawberry to be seen, while every man of fashion's table in London is covered with them; and all the shops of Covent Garden and St. James's Street hang out their luxurious temptations of fruit, to prove the proximity of summer, and the advantages of industrious cultivation. Our eating pleased me more at every town than this; where, however, a man might live very well I believe for sixpence a day, and lodge for twenty pounds a year; and whoever has no attachment to religion, friends, or country, no prejudices to plague his neighbours with, and no dislike to take the world as it goes for six or seven years of his life, may spend them profitably at Rome, if either his business or his pleasure be made out of the works of art, as an income of two, or indeed of one hundred pounds per annum will purchase a man more refined delights of that kind here than as many thousands in England: nor need he want society at the first houses—palaces one ought to call them—as Italians measure no man's merit by the weight of his purse; they know how to reverence even poverty, and soften all its sorrows with an appearance of respect when they find it unfortunately connected with noble birth. His own country-folk's neglect, as they pass through, would indeed be likely enough to disturb his felicity and lessen the kindness of his Roman friends, who, having no idea of a person's being shunned for any other possible reason except the want of a pedigree, would conclude that his must be essentially deficient, and lament their having laid out so many caresses on an impostor.

The air of the city is unwholesome to foreigners, but if they pass the first year, the remainder goes well enough. Many English seem very healthy who are established here without even the smallest intention of returning home to Great Britain, for which place we are setting out to-morrow, 19th April, 1786, and quit a town that still retains so many just pretences to be styled the first among the cities of the earth, to which almost as many strangers are now attracted by curiosity as were dragged thither by violence in the first stage of its dominion, impelled by superstitious zeal in the second. The rage for antiquities now seems to have spread its contagion of connoisseurship over all those people whose predecessors tore down, levelled, and destroyed, or buried underground, their statues, pictures, every work of art; Poles, Russians, Swedes, and Germans innumerable flock daily hither in this age to admire with rapture the remains of those very fabrics which their own barbarous ancestors pulled down ten centuries ago, and give for the head of a Livia, a Probus, or Gallienus, what emperors and queens could not then use with any efficacy for the preservation of their own persons, now grown sacred by rust and valuable from their difficulty to be deciphered. The English were wont to be the only travellers of Europe, the only dupes, too, in this way; but desire of distinction is diffused among all the northern nations, and our Romans here have it more in their power, with that prudence to assist them which it is said they do not want, if not to conquer their neighbours once again, at least to ruin them, by dint of digging up their dead heroes, and calling in the assistance of their old pagan deities, now useful to them in a new manner, and ever propitious to this city.

CHAPTER XI

RETURN TO MILAN

Loretto—The Santa Casa—Ancona—Inns—Convicts—Vegetation—Verona—Bad Roads—Mantua—A Penance—Piacenza—Heat—Milan—Reforms—Processions—Sincerity—Varieties of Character.

Loretto.

THE richest treasures of Europe stand in the most delicious district of it. The number of beggars offended me, because I hold it next to impossibility that they should want in a country so luxuriantly abundant; and their prostrations, as they kneel and kiss the ground before you, are more calculated to produce disgust from British travellers than compassion. Nor can I think these vagabonds distressed in earnest, at this time above all others, when their sovereign provides them with employment on the beautiful new road he is making, and insists on their being well paid who are found willing to work. But the town itself of Loretto claims my attention, so clear are its streets, so numerous and cheerful and industrious are its inhabitants; one would think they had resolved to rob passengers of the trite remark which the sight of dead wealth always inspires, that the money might be better bestowed upon the living poor. For here are very few poor families, and fewer idlers than one expects to see in a place where not business but devotion is the leading characteristic. So quiet, too, and inoffensive are the folks here, that scarcely any robberies or murders, or any but very petty infringements of the law, are ever committed among them. Yet people grieve to see that wealth collected which once diffused would certainly make many happy, and those treasures lying dead which well dispersed might keep thousands alive.

It was curious to see the devotees drag themselves round the holy house upon their knees; but the Santa Scala at Rome had shown me the same operation performed with more difficulty, and a written injunction at bottom, less agreeable for Italians to comply with than any possible prostration, viz., that no one should spit as he went up or down, except in his pocket-handkerchief. The lamps which burn night and day before the black image here at Loretto are of solid gold, and there is such a crowd of them I scarcely could see the figure for my own part; and, that one may see still less, the attendant canons throw a veil over one's face going in.

The confessionals, where all may be heard in their own language, is not peculiar to this church; I met with it somewhere else, but have forgotten where, though I much esteemed the establishment. It is very entertaining here, too, to see inscriptions in twelve different tongues, giving an account of the miraculous removal and arrival here of the Santa Casa. I was delighted with the Welsh one; and our conductor said there came not unfrequently pilgrims from the Vale of Llwydd, who in their turns told the wonders of their holy well.

I told a learned ecclesiastic at Rome that we should return home by the way of Loretto.

'There is no need,' said he, 'to caution a native of your island against credulity, but pray do not believe that we are ourselves satisfied with the tale you will read there. No man of learning but knows that Adrian destroyed every trace and vestige of Christianity that he could find in the East, and he was acute and diligent and powerful. The Empress Helena long after him, with piety that equalled even his profaneness, could never hear of this holy house; how, then, should it have waited till so many long years after Jesus Christ? Truth is, Pope Boniface VIII., who canonized St. Louis, who instituted the jubilee, who quarrelled with Philippe le Bel about a new crusade, and who at last fretted himself to death, though he had conquered all his enemies, because he feared some loss of power to the Church —desired to give mankind a new object of attention, and encouraged an old visionary, in the year 1296, to propagate the tale he half-believed himself—how the blessed Virgin had appeared to him and related the story you will read upon the walls, which was then first committed to paper. In consequence of this intelligence, Boniface sent men into the East that he could best depend upon, and they brought back just such particulars as would best please the Pope; and in those days you can scarce think how quick the blaze of superstition caught and communicated itself: no one wished to deny what his neighbour was willing to believe, and what he himself would then have gained no credit by contradicting. Positive evidence of what the house really was, or whence it came, it was in a few years impossible to obtain; nor did Boniface VIII. know it himself, I suppose, much less the old visionary who first set the matter a-going. Meantime, the house itself has no foundation, whatever the story may have. It is a very singular house, as you may see; it has been venerated by the best and wisest among Christians now for five hundred years; even the Turks, who have the same method of honouring their prophet with gifts as we do the Virgin Mary, respect the very name of Loretto. Why, then, should the place be to any order of thinking beings a just object of insult or mockery?'

Here he ended his discourse, the recollection of which never left me whilst we remained at the place.

But we must leave Loretto, to proceed along the side of this lovely sea, hearing the pilgrims sing most sweetly as they go along in troops towards the town, with now and then a female voice peculiarly distinguished from the rest. By this means a new image is presented to one's mind; the sight of such figures, too, half alarm the fancy, and give an air of distance from England which nothing has hitherto inspired half so strongly. This charming Adriatic gulf, beside, though more than delicious to drive by, does not, like the Mediterranean, convey homeish or familiar ideas; one feels that it belongs exclusively to Venice; one knows that ancient Greece is on the opposite shore.

Here are plenty of nightingales, but they do not sing as well as in Hertfordshire. Birds gain in colour as you approach the tropic, but they lose in song; under the torrid zone I have heard they never sing at all; with us in England the latest leave off by midsummer, when the work of incubation goes forward and the parental duties begin. The nightingale, too, chooses the coolest hour, and, though I have yet heard her in Italy only early in the mornings, Virgil knew she sung in the night. To hear birds, it is, however, indispensably necessary that there should be high trees, and except in these parts of Italy, and those about Genoa and Siena, no timber of any good growth can I find. The *roccolo*, too, and other methods taken to catch small birds, which many delight in eating and more in taking, lessen the quantity of natural music vexatiously enough; while gaudy insects ill supply their place, and sharpen their stings at pleasure when deprived of their greatest enemies. We are here less tormented than usual, however, while the prospects are varied so that every look produces a new and beautiful landscape.

Ancona.

Ancona is a town perfectly agreeable to strangers, from the good humour with which every nation is received and every religion patiently endured.

Here are good fish, and, to say true, everything eatable as much in perfection as possible. I could never since I arrived at Turin find real cause of complaint—serious complaint I mean—except at that savage-looking place called Radicofani, and some other petty town in Tuscany near Siena, where I ate too many eggs and grapes because there was nothing else.

Nice accommodations must not be looked for, and need not be regretted, where so much amusement during the day gives one good disposition to sleep sound at night. The worst is, men and women, servants and masters, must often mess together; but if one frets about such things, it is better stay at home. The Italians like travelling in England no better than the English do travelling in Italy; whilst an exorbitant expense is incurred by the journey, not well repaid to them by the waiters' white chitterlins, tambour waistcoats, and independent 'No, sir,' echoed round a well-furnished inn or tavern, which puts them but in the place of Socrates at the fair, who cried out: 'How many things have these people gathered together that I do not want!' A noble Florentine complained exceedingly to me once of the English hotels, where he was made to help pay for those good gold watches the fellows who attended him drew from their pockets; so he set up his quarters comically enough at the Waggoners' Full Moon, upon the old bridge at Bath, to be quit of the *schiavitù,* as he called it, of living like a gentleman, 'where,' says he, 'I am not known to be one.' The truth is, a continental nobleman can have little heart of a country where, to be treated as a man of fashion, he must absolutely behave as such. His rank is ascertained at home, and people's deportment to him regulated by long-established customs; nor can it be supposed flattering to its prejudices to feel himself jostled in the street or driven against upon the road by a rich trader while he is contriving the cheapest method of going to look over his manufactory. Wealth diffused makes all men comfortable and leaves no man splendid, gives everybody two dishes, but nobody two hundred. Objects of show are therefore unfrequent in England, and a foreigner who travels through our country in search of positive sights will, after much money spent, go home but poorly entertained. 'There is neither quaresima,' will he say, 'nor carnovale in any sense of the word among those insipid islanders.' For he who does not love our government, and taste our manners which result from it, can never be delighted in England; while the inhabitants of our nation may always be amused in theirs, without any esteem of it at all.

I know not how Ancona produced all these tedious reflections; it is a trading-place and a seaport town.

Men working in chains upon the new mole did not please me, though, and their insensibility shocks one.

'Give a poor thief something, master,' says one impudent fellow. 'Son stato ladro, padrone'*—with a grin.

That such people should be corrupt or coarse, however, is no wonder. What surprised me most was, that when one of our company spoke of his conduct to a man of the town:

'Why, what would you have, sir?' replies the person applied to. 'When the poor creature is castigato, it is enough sure; no need to make him be melancholy, too;' and added, with true Italian good-nature, 'Siamo tutti peccatori.'†

Padua.

We dined at a lovely villa belonging to an amiable friend upon the margin of the river, where the kind embraces of the Padrona di Casa, added to the fragrance of her garden, and the sweet breath of oxen drawing in her team, revived me once more to the enjoyment of cheerful conversation, by restoring my natural health, and proving beyond a possibility of doubt that my late disorder was of the putrid

---

* 'I am a light-fingered fellow, master.'
† 'We are all sinners, you know.'

kind. We dined in a grotto-like room, and partook the evening refreshments—cake, ice and lemonade—under a tree by the river-side, whilst my own feelings reminded me of the sailors' delight, described in Anson's voyages, when they landed at Juan Fernandez. Night was best disposed of in the barge, and I observed, as we entered Padua early in the morning, how surprisingly quick had been the progress of summer; but in these countries vegetation is so rapid, that everything makes haste to come and more to go. Scarce have you tasted green peas or strawberries before they are out of season; and if you do not swallow your pleasures, as Madame la Présidente said, you have a chance to miss of getting any pleasures at all. Here is no mediocrity in anything, no moderate weather, no middle rank of life, no twilight; whatever is not night is day, and whatever is not love is hatred; and that the English should eat peaches in May and green peas in October sounds to Italian ears as a miracle; they comfort themselves, however, by saying that they must be very insipid, while we know that fruits forced by strong fire are, at least many of them, higher in flavour than those produced by sun—the pineapple particularly, which West Indians confess eats better with us than with them. Figs and cherries, however, defy a hothouse, and grapes raised by art are worth little except for show; peaches, nectarines, and ananas are the glory of a British gardener, and no country but England can show such. Our morning, passed at the villa of the Senator Quirini, set us on this train of thinking, for every culled excellence adorned it, and brought to my mind Voltaire's description of Pococurante in 'Candide,' false only in the ostentation, and there the character fails, misled by a French idea that pleasure is nothing without the delight of showing that you are pleased, like the old adage or often quoted passage about learning:

> 'Scire tuum nihil est, nisi te scire hoc sciat alter.'*

A Venetian has no such notions; by force of mind and dint of elegance inherent in it, he pleases himself first, and finds everybody else delighted of course, nor would quit his own country except for paradise; while an English nobleman clumps his trees and twists his river to comply with his neighbour's taste, when perhaps he has none of his own, feels disgusted with all he has done, and runs away to live in Italy.

The evening of this day was spent at the theatre, where I was glad the audience were no better pleased, for the plaudits of an Italian Platea at an

* 'Thy knowledge is nothing till other men know that thou knowest it.'

air they like, when one's nerves are weak and the weather very hot, are all but totally insupportable.

Verona.

The road from Padua hither is a vile one; one can scarcely make twenty miles a-day in any part of the Venetian state. Its senators, accustomed to water-carriage, have little care for us who go by land. The Palanzuola way is worse, however, and I am glad once more to see sweet Verona.

Petruchio and Catharine might easily have met with all the adventures related by Grumio on their journey thither, but when once arrived she should have been contented. This city is as lovely as ever, more so than it was last April twelvemonth, when the spring was sullen and backward; every hill now glows with the gay produce of summer, and every valley smiles with plenty expected or pleasure possessed.

We took leave of our learned friends here with concern, but hope to see them again and tread the stucco floors so prettily mottled and variegated, they look like the cold mock-turtle soup exactly, which London pastrycooks keep in their shops ready for immediate use.

What an odd thing is custom! Here is weather

to fry one in, yet after exercise, and in a state of the most violent perspiration, no consequences follow the use of iced beverages, except the sense of pleasure resulting from them at the moment. Should a Bath belle indulge in such luxury after dancing down forty couple at Mr. Tyson's ball, we should expect to hear next day of her surfeit at least, if not of her sudden death. Lying-in ladies take the same liberty with their constitutions, and say that no harm comes of it; and, when I tell them how differently we manage in England, cry, ' Mi pare che dev' essere schiavitù grande in quel paese della benedetta libertà.'* Fine muslin linen nicely got up is, however, say they, one of the things to be produced only in Great Britain, and much do our Italian ladies admire it, though they look very charmingly with much less trouble taken. I lent one lady at some place, I remember, my maid, to show her, as she so much wished it, how the operation of clear-starching was performed; but as soon as it began, she laughed at the superfluous fatigue, as she called it, and her servants crossed themselves in every corner of the room with wonder that such niceties should be required. Well they might! for I caught a great tall fellow ironing his lady's best

---

* 'Methinks there seems to be much slavery required from those who inhabit your fine free country of England.'

neck-handkerchief with the warming-pan here at Padua very quietly; and she was a woman of quality, too, and looked as lovely, when the toilette was once performed, as if much more attention had been bestowed upon it.

Mantua.

We passed through Mantua the 18th of June, where nothing much attracted my notice, except a female figure in the street, veiled from head to foot and covered wholly in black; she walked backward and forward along the same portion of the same street from one to three o'clock, in the heat of the burning sun, her hand held out; but when I, more from curiosity than any better motive, put money in it, she threw it silently away, and the beggars picked it up, while she held her hand again as before. This conduct in any town of England would be deemed madness or mischief; the woman would be carried before a magistrate to give an account of herself, should the mob forbear to uncase her till they came; or some charitable person would seize and carry her home, fill her pockets with money, and coax her out·of the anecdotes of her past life to put in the magazine; her print would be published, and many engravers struggle for its profits, the name at bottom 'Annabella, or the Sable Matron';

while novels would be written without end, and the circulating libraries would lend them out all the livelong day. Things are differently carried on, however, at Mantua. I asked one shopkeeper, and she gravely replied, 'Per divozione,' and took no further notice; another (to my inquiries, which appeared to him far odder than the woman's conduct) said the lady was possibly doing a little penance; that he had not minded her till I spoke, but that perhaps it might be some woman of fashion, who, having refused a poor person roughly on some occasion, was condemned by her confessor to try for a couple of hours what begging was, and learn humanity from experience of evil. The idea charmed me; while the man coolly said all this was only his conjecture, but that such things were done too often to attract attention, and hoped such virtue was not rare enough to excite wonder. My just applause of such sentiments was stopped by the laquais de place calling me to dinner, when he informed me that he had asked about the person whose behaviour struck me so, and could now tell me all there was to be known. She was a lady of quality, he said, who had lost a dear friend on that day some years past, and that she wore black for two hours ever since upon its anniversary; but that she would now change her dress, and I should see her in the evening at the opera. My recollecting that if this were her case I ought to have been keeping her company (as no one ever lost a friend so dear to them as was my incomparable mother, who likewise left me to mourn her loss on this day thirteen years) spoiled my appetite, and took from me all power of meeting the lady at the theatre.

Piacenza.

Piacenza we found to offer us few objects of attention. An improvisatore, and not a very bad one, amused that time which would otherwise have been passed in lamenting our paucity of entertainment, while his artful praises of England put me in good humour, spite of the weather, which is too hot to bear. With all our lamentations about the heat, however, here is no cicala on the trees, or lucciola in the hedges, as at Florence; the days are a little longer, too, and the crepuscule less abrupt in its departure. How often, upon the Ponte della Trinitá, have I secretly regretted the long-drawn evenings of an English summer, when the dewy nightfall refreshes the air, and silent dusk brings on a train of meditations uninspired by Italian skies! In this decided country all that is not broad day is dark night, all that is not loud mirth is penitence and grief; when the rain falls, it falls in a torrent;

when the sun shines, it glows like a burning-glass ; where the people are rich, they stick gems in their very walls and make their chimneys of amethyst ; where they are poor, they clasp your knees in an agony of pinching want and display diseases which cannot be a day survived !

Talking on about Italy in which there is no mediocrity, and of England in which there is nothing else, we arrived at Lodi, where I began to rejoice in hearing the people cry ' No' cor' altr' ' again in reply to our commands, because we were now once more returned to the district and dialect of dear Milan, where we have cool apartments and warm friends, and where, after an absence of fifteen months, we shall again see those acquaintance with whom we lived once before—a sensation always delightfully soothing, even when one returns to less amiable scenes, and less productive of innocent pleasure than these have been to me.

Milan, 21st June, 1786.

After rejoicing over my house and my friends, after asking a hundred questions and hearing a hundred stories of those long left, after reciprocating common civilities and talking over common topics, we observed how much the general look of Milan was improved in these last fifteen months—how the town was become neater, the ordinary people smarter, the roads round their city mended, and the beggars cleared away from the streets. We did not find, however, that the people we talked to were at all charmed with these new advantages—their convents demolished, their processions put an end to, the number of their priests of course contracted, and their church plate carried by cart-loads to the mint; holidays forbidden, and every saint's name erased from the calendar, excepting only St. Peter and St. Paul; whilst those shopkeepers who worked for monasteries, and those musicians who sung or played in oratorios, are left to find employment how they can—cloud the countenance of all, and justly, as such sudden and rough reforms shock the feelings of the multitude, offend the delicacy of the nobles, make a general stagnation of business and of pleasure in a country where both depend upon religious functions, and terrify the clergy into no ill-grounded apprehensions of being found in a few years more wholly useless, and as such dismissed. Well, whatever is done hastily can scarcely be done quite well, and wherever much is done a great part of it will doubtless be done wrong. A considerable portion of all this, however, will be confessed useful, and even necessary, when the hour of violence on one side, and prejudice on the other, is passed away, as the fire of London has been found beneficial by those who live in the newly-restored town. Meantime, I think the present precipitation indecent enough for my own part; a thousand little errors would burn out of themselves were they suffered to die quietly away, and, when the morning breaks in naturally, it is superfluous as awkward to put the stars out with one's fingers, like the Hours in Guercino's 'Aurora.'* Whoever, therefore, will be at the pains a little to pick their principles, not grasp them by the bunch, will find as many unripe at one end, I believe, as there are rotten at the other; for could we see these hasty innovators erecting public schools for the instruction of the poor, or public workhouses for their employment—did they unlock the treasure-house of true religion by publishing the Bible in every dialect of their dominions, and oblige their clergy to read it with the souls committed to their charge—I should have a better idea of their sincerity and disinterested zeal for God's glory than they give by tearing down His statues, or those of His blessed Virgin Mother, which Carlo Borromeo set up.

The folly of hanging churches with red damask would surely fade away of itself among people of

* In the fine ceiling of the Palazzo Ludovigi, at Rome, the Hours which surround Aurora's chariot are employed in extinguishing the stars with their hands.

good sense and good taste, who could not long be simple enough to suppose that concealing Greek architecture with such transient finery, and giving to God's house the air of a tattered theatre, could in any wise promote His service or their salvation. Many superstitious and many unmeaning ceremonies do die off every day, because unsupported by reason or religion. Dr. Carpanni, a learned lawyer, told me but to-day that here in Lombardy they had a custom, no longer ago than in his father's time, of burying a great lord or possessor of lands with a ceremony of killing on his grave the favourite horse, dog, etc., that he delighted in when alive—a usage borrowed from the Oriental pagans, who burn even the widows of the deceased upon their funeral pile; and among our monuments in Westminster Abbey, set up in the days of darkness, I have minded now and then the hawk and greyhound of a nobleman lying in marble at his feet. Some of our antiquarians should tell us if they killed them.

Another odd affinity strikes me. Half a century ago there was an annual procession at Shrewsbury, called by way of pre-eminence Shrewsbury Show, when a handsome young girl of about twelve years old rode round the town and wished prosperity to every trade assembled at the fair. I forget what else made the amusement interesting, but have heard my mother tell of the particular beauty of some wench, who was ever after called the queen, because she had been carried in triumph as such on the day of Shrewsbury Show. Now, if nobody gives a better derivation of that old custom, it may perhaps be found a dreg of the Romish superstition which as many years ago, in various parts of Italy, prompted people to dress up a pretty girl, on the 25th of March, or other season dedicated to the Virgin, and carry her in procession about the streets, singing litanies to her, etc., and ending in profaneness of admiration a day begun in idleness and folly. At Rome, however, no such indecorous absurdities are encouraged. We saw a beautiful figure of the Madonna, dressed from a picture of Guido Reni, borne about one day, but no human creature in the street offered to kneel, or gave one the slightest reason to say or suppose that she was worshipped. Some sweet hymns were sung in her praise as the procession moved slowly on, but no impropriety could I discern, who watched with great attention.

Our good Italians here will not condescend to live a lie, if now and then they scruple not to tell one. No man in this country pretends either to tenderness or to indifference when he feels no disposition to be indifferent or tender, and so removed are they from all affectation of sensibility or of refinement, that when a conceited Englishman starts back in pretended rapture from a Raphael he has perhaps little taste for, it is difficult to persuade these sincerer people that his transports are possibly put on only to deceive some of his countrymen who stand by, and who, if he took no notice of so fine a picture, would laugh and say he had been throwing his time away, without making even the common and necessary improvements expected from every gentleman who travels through Italy; yet surely it is a choice delight to live where the everlasting scourge held over London and Bath, of What will they think? and What will they say? has no existence; and to reflect that I have now sojourned near two years in Italy, and scarcely can name one conceited man or one affected woman with whom, in any rank of life, I have been in the least connected.

There is a natural loyalty among the Lombards which oppression can scarcely extinguish or tyranny destroy, and, as I have said a thousand times, they pretend to love no one; they do love their rulers, and rather grieve than growl at the afflictions caused by their rapacity.

I was told that I should find few discriminations

of character in Italy, but the contrary proves true, and I do not wonder at it. Among those people who, by being folded or driven all together in flocks as the French are, with one fashion to serve for the whole society, a man may easily contract a similarity of manners by rubbing down each asperity of character against his nearest neighbour, no less plastic than himself; but here, where there is little apprehension of ridicule and little spirit of imitation, monotonous tediousness is almost sure to be escaped. The very word 'polite' comes from 'polish,' I suppose; and at Paris, the place where you enjoy *le veritable vernis St. Martin* in perfection, the people can scarcely be termed polished, or even varnished; they are glazed, and everything slides off the *exterieur* of course, leaving the heart untouched. It is the same thing with other productions of nature; in caverns we see petrifactions shooting out in angular and eccentric forms, because in Castleton Hole dame Nature has fair play; while the broad beach at Brighthelmstone, evermore battered by the same ocean, exhibits only a heap of round pebbles, and those round pebbles all alike.

CHAPTER XII

LAGO MAGGIORE—RETURN TO VERONA

Varese—Diversions on the Lake—Untidy Mansions—Love of Society—Lugano—A Republican Cicerone—Bergamo—Milan—Dislike of Mimicry—A Spanish Grandee—Dialects—Verona—Contemporary Singing—Farewell to Verona.

Varese.

WE have got a country house for the remaining part of the hot weather upon the confines of the Milanese dominions, where Switzerland first begins to bow her bleak head and soften gradually in the sunshine of Italian fertility. From every walk and villa round this delightful spot one sees an assemblage of beauties rarely to be met with; and there is a resemblance in it to the Vale of Llwydd, which makes it still more interesting to me. But we have obtained leave to spend a week of our destined Villeggiatura at the Borromean Palace, situated in the middle of Lago Maggiore, on the island so truly termed Isola Bella, every step to which from our villa at Varese teems with new beauties, and only wants the sea to render it, in point of mere landscape, superior to anything we have seen yet.

Our manner of living here is positively like nothing real, and the fanciful description of Oriental magnificence, with Seged's retirement in the Rambler to his palace on the Lake Dambea, is all I ever read that could come in competition with it; for here is one barge full of friends from Milan, another carrying a complete band of thirteen of the best musicians in Italy, to amuse ourselves and them with concerts every evening upon the water by moonlight, while the inhabitants of these elysian regions who live upon the banks come down in crowds to the shores, glad to receive additional delight, where satiety of pleasure seems the sole evil to be dreaded.

It is well known that the wild mountains of Savoy, the rich plains of Lombardy, the verdant pastures of Piedmont, and the pointed Alps of Switzerland, form the limits of Lago Maggiore, where, upon a naked rock—torn, I trust, from some surrounding hill, or happily thrown up in the middle of the water by a subterranean volcano—the Count Borromeo, in the year 1613, began to carry earth and lay out a pretty garden, which from that day has been perpetually improving, till an appearance of Eastern grandeur which it now wears is rendered still more charming by all the studied elegance of art and the conveniences of common life. The palace is constructed as if to realize Johnson's ideas in his 'Prince of Abyssinia.' The garden consists of ten terraces, the walls of which are completely covered with orange, lemon, and cedrati trees, whose glowing colours and whose fragrant scent are easily discerned at a considerable distance, and the perfume particularly often reaches as far as to the opposite shore; nor are standards of the same plants wanting. I measured one, not the largest in the grove, which had been planted one hundred and five years; it was a full yard and a quarter round. There were forty-six of them set near each other, and formed a delightful shade. The cedrati fruit grows as large as a late romana melon with us in England; and everything one sees, and everything one hears, and everything one tastes, brings to one's mind the Fortunate Islands and the Golden Age. Walks, woods and terraces within the island, and a prospect of unequalled variety without, make this a kind of fairy habitation, so like something one has seen represented on theatres, that my female companion cried out, as we approached the place, 'If we go any nearer now, I am sure it will all vanish into air.' There is solidity enough, however—a little village consisting of eighteen fishermen's houses, and a pretty church, with a dozen of well-grown poplars before it, together with the palace and garden, compose the territory, which commodiously contains two hundred and fifty souls, as the circuit is somewhat more than a measured mile and a half, but not two miles in all; and we have cannons to guard our Calypso-like dominion, for which Count Borromeo pays tribute to the King of Sardinia, but has himself the right of raising men upon the mainland, and of coining money at Macan, a little town amid the hollows of these rocks, which present their irregular fronts to the lake in a manner surprisingly beautiful. He has three other islets on the same water for change of amusement, of which that named La Superiore is covered with a hamlet, and L'Isola Madre with a wood full of game, guinea fowl, and common poultry; a summerhouse beside, furnished with chintz, and containing so many apartments, that I am told the uncle of the present possessor, having quarrelled with his wife, and resolving in a pet to leave the world, shut himself up on that little spot of earth, and never touched the continent, as I may call it, for the last seventeen years of his life. Let me add that he had there his church and his chaplain, three musical professors in constant pay, and a pretty yacht to row or sail and fetch in friends, physicians, etc., from the mainland. His nephew has not the same taste at all, seldom spending more than a week, and that only once a-year, among his islands, which are kept, however, quite in a princely style—the family crest, a unicorn made in white marble, and of colossal greatness, proudly overlooking ten broad terraces, which rise in a pyramidal form from the water, each wall richly covered with orange and lemon trees, and every parapet concealed under thickly-flowering shrubs of incessant variety, as if every climate had been culled to adorn this tiny spot. More than a hundred beds are made in the palace, which has likewise a grotto-floor of infinite ingenuity, and beautiful from being happily contrasted against the general splendour of the house itself. I have seen no such effort of what we call taste since I left England as these apartments on a level with the lake exhibit, being all roofed and wainscoted with well-disposed shell-work, and decorated with fountains in a lively and pleasing manner.

Some large history pieces adorn the walls of the vast room we dine in, where, though we never sit down fewer than twenty or twenty-five people to table, all seem lost from the greatness of its size, till the concert fills it in the evening.

It is the garden, however, more than the palace

which deserves description. He who has the care
of it was born upon the island, and never strayed
further than four miles, he tells me, from the borders
of his master's lake. Sure, he must think the fall of
man a fable; he lives in Eden still. How much
must such a fellow be confounded, could he be
carried blindfolded in the midst of winter to London
or to Paris, and set down in Fleet Street or Rue St.
Honoré! That he understands his business so as to
need no tuition from the inhabitants of either city,
may be seen by a fig-tree which I found here ingrafted on a lemon; both bear fruit at the same
moment, whilst a vine curls up the stem of the
lemon-tree, dangling her grapes in that delicious
company with apparent satisfaction to herself.
Another inoculation of a moss-rose upon an orange
and a third of a carnation upon a cedrati tree, gave
me new knowledge of what the gardener's art, aided
by a happy climate, could perform. But when
rowing round the lake with our band of music
yesterday, we touched at a country seat upon the
side which joins the Milanese dominion, and I found
myself presented with currants and gooseberries by
a kind family, who, having made their fortune in
Amsterdam, had imbibed some Dutch ideas.

We returned to our enchanted palace with music

playing by our side. I never saw a party of pleasure carried on so happily. The weather was singularly bright and clear, the moon at full; the French horns, breaking the silence of the night, invited echo to answer them. The nine days (and we enjoyed seventeen or eighteen hours out of every twenty-four) seemed nine minutes. When we came home to our country-house in the Varesotto, verses and sonnets saluted our arrival, and congratulated our wedding-day.

Of the noblemen's seats in the neighbourhood it may indeed be remarked that, however spacious the house, and however splendid the furniture may prove upon examination, however pompous the garden may be to the first glance, and the terraces however magnificent—spiders are seldom excluded from the mansion or weeds from the pleasure-ground of the possessor. A climate so warm would afford some excuse for this nastiness, could one observe the inhabitants were discomposed at such an effect from a good cause, or if one could flatter one's self that they themselves were hurt at it; but when they gravely display an embroidered bed or counterpane worthy of Arachne's fingers before her metamorphosis, covered over by her present labours, who can forbear laughing? The gardener in two minutes arriving to assist you up slopes, all flourishing with cat's-tail and poppy, while your friends cry, 'Here, this is nature!—is it not?—pure nature!' 'Tutto naturale si, secondo l'uso Inglese.'*

But I am disturbed from writing my book by the good-humoured gaiety of our cheerful friends, with whom we never sit down fewer than fourteen or fifteen to table, I think, and surely never rise from it without many a genuine burst of honest merriment, undisguised by affectation, unfettered by restraint. Our gentlemen make improviso rhymes and cut comical faces, go out to the field after dinner and play at a sort of blind-man's-buff, which they call breaking the pan; nor do the low ones in company arrange their minds, as I see, in compliment to the high ones, but tell their opinions with a freedom I little expected to find. Mixed society is very rare among them—almost unknown, it seems—but when they do mix at a country place like this, the great are kind, to do them justice, and the little not servile. They are wise indeed in making society easy to them, for no human being suffers solitude so ill as does an Italian. An English lady once made me observe that a cat never purrs when she is alone, let her have what meat and warmth she will; I

* 'All so natural and pretty—quite in the English style.'

think these social-spirited Milanese are like her, for they can hardly believe that there is existing a person who would not willingly prefer any company to none. When we were at the islands three weeks ago:

'A charming place,' says one of our companions —' Cio é con un mondo d'amici cosi.'*

'But with one's own family, methinks,' said I, 'and a good library of books, and this sweet lake to bathe in——'

'Oh!' cried they all at once, 'Dio ne liberi.'†

This is national character.

Why there are no birds of the watery kind, coots, wild ducks, cargeese, upon these lakes, nobody informs me; I have been often told that of Geneva swarms with them, and it is but a very few miles off. Our people, though, have little care to ascertain such matters, and no desire at all to investigate effects and causes; those who study among them study classic authors and learn rhetoric. Poetry, too, is by no means uncultivated at Milan, where the Abate Parini's satires are admirable, and so esteemed by those who themselves know very well how to write and how to judge. Common philosophy (la physique, as the French call it), geography, astronomy, che-

* 'That is, with a heap of friends about one in this manner.'
† 'Oh! God keep one from that.'

mistry, are oddly left behind somehow; and it is to their ignorance of these matters that I am apt to impute Italian credulity, to which every wonder is welcome.

Lugano.

We have now passed one day in Switzerland, rowing to the little town Lugano over its pretty lake. A fanciful traveller might be tempted to think he could discern some streaks of liberty in the manners of the people, if it were but in the innkeeper at whose house we dined; this may, however, be merely my own prejudice, and somebody told me it was so.

We were shown on one side the water as we went across a small place called Campioni, which is *feudo imperiale*, and governed by the Padre Abate of a neighbouring convent, who has power even over the lives of his subjects for six years, at the expiration of which term another despot of the day is chosen—appointed, I should have said—and the last returns to his original state, amenable, however, for any very shocking thing he may have done during the course of his dictatorship; and no complaint has been ever made yet of any such governor so circumstanced and appointed, whose conduct is commonly but too mild and clement. This I thought worth remarking, as consolatory to one's feelings.

Lugano meantime scorns absolute authority. Our cicerone there, in reply to the question—asked in Italy three times a day, I believe—'Che Principe fà qui la sua residenza?'* replied that they were plagued with no *principi* at all, while the thirteen cantons protected all their subjects; and though, as the man expressed it, only half of them were Christians, and the other half Protestants, no church or convent had ever wanted respect, while their town regularly received a monthly governor from every canton, and was perfectly contented with this ambulatory dominion. Here was the first gallows I have seen these two years. They have a pretty commerce, too, at Lugano for the size of the place, and the shopkeepers show that officiousness and attention seldom observed in arbitrary States, where

'Content, the bane of industry,'

soon leads people to neglect the trouble of getting for the pleasure of spending their money. One therefore sees the inhabitants of Italian cities for the most part merry and cheerful, or else pious and penitent; little attentive to their shops, but easily disposed to loiter under their mistress's window with a guitar, or rove about the streets at night with a pretty girl under their arm, singing as they go, or squeaking with a droll accent if it is the time for

* 'What prince makes his residence here?'

masquerades. Fraud, avarice, ambition, are the vices of republican States and a cold climate; idleness, sensuality, and revenge are the weeds of a warm country and monarchical governments. If these people are not good, they at least wish they were better; they do not applaud their own conduct when their passions carry them too far. They beat their bosoms at the foot of a crucifix in the street with no more hypocrisy than they beat a tambourine there—perhaps with no more effect neither, if no alteration of behaviour succeeds their contrition; yet when an Englishman (who is probably more ashamed of repenting than of sinning) accuses them of false pretensions to pious fervour, he wrongs them, and would do well to repent himself.

Bergamo.

Bergamo is built up a steep hill, like Lansdown Road at Bath—the buildings not so regular—the prospect not inferior, but of a different kind, resembling that one sees from Wrotham Hill in Kent, but richer, and presenting a variety beyond credibility, when it is premised that scarce any water can be seen, and that the plains of Lombardy are low and flat. Within the eye, however, one may count all the original blessings bestowed on human kind—corn, wine, oil, and fruit—the enclosures being small, too, and the trees *touffu,* as the French call it. No parterre was ever more beautifully disposed than are the fields surveyed from the summit of the hill, where stands the marquis's palace, elegantly sheltered by a still higher rising ground behind it, and commanding from every window of its stately front a view of prodigious extent and almost unmatched beauty, as the diversification of colouring reminds one of nothing but the fine pavement at the Roman Pantheon, so curiously intersected are the patches of grass and grain, flax and vines, arable and tilth, in this happy disposition of earth and its most valuable products; while not a hedge fails to afford perfume that fills the very air with fragrance, from the sweet jessamine that, twisting through it, lends a weak support to the wild grapes, which, dangling in clusters, invite ten thousand birds of every European species, I believe, below the size of a pigeon. Nor is the taking of these creatures by the *roccolo* to be left out from among the amusements of Brescian and Bergamasc nobility, nor is the eating of them when taken to be despised. Beccaficos and ortolans are here in high perfection, and it was from these northern districts of Italy, I trust, that Vitellius and all the classic gluttons of antiquity got their curious dishes of singing-bird pie, etc. The rich scent of melons at every cottage door is another delicious proof of the climate's fertility and opulence—

> 'Where every sense is lost in every joy,'

as Hughes expresses it, and where, in the delightful villa of our highly accomplished acquaintance, the Marquis of Aracieli, we have passed ten days in all the pleasures which wit could invent, money purchase, or friendship bestow. The last nobleman who resided here, father to the present lord, was cavalier servente to the immortal Clelia Borromeo, whose virtues and varieties of excellence would fill a volume.

Could I clear my head of prejudice for such talents as I find here, and my heart of partial regard, which is in reality but grateful friendship, justly due from me for so many favours received—could I forget that we are now once more in the state of Venice, where everything assumes an air of cheerfulness unknown to other places, I might perhaps perceive that the fair at Bergamo differs little from a fair in England, except that these cattle are whiter and ours larger. ' How a score of good ewes now?' as Master Shallow says ; but I really did ask the price of a pair of good strong oxen for work, and heard it was ten zecchines, about half the price given at Blackwater; but ours are stouter and capable of rougher service. It is strange to me where these creatures are kept all the rest of the year, for, except at fair-time, one very seldom sees them, unless in actual employment of carting, ploughing, etc. Nothing is so little animated by the sight of living creatures as an Italian prospect. No sheep upon their hills, no cattle grazing in their meadows, no water-fowl, swans, ducks, etc., upon their lakes; and, when you leave Lombardy, no birds flying in the air, save only from time to time, betwixt Florence and Bologna, a solitary kite soaring over the surly Apennines, and breaking the immense void which fatigues the eye; a ragged lad or wench, too, now and then leading a lean cow to pick among the hedges, has a melancholy appearance, the more so as it is always fast held by a string, and struggles in vain to get loose. These, however, are only consequences of luxuriant plenty, for where the farmer makes four harvests of his grass, and every other speck of ground is profitably covered with grain, vines, etc., all possibility of open pasturage is precluded. Horses, too, so ornamental in an English landscape, will never be seen loose in an Italian one, as they are all *chevaux entiers*, and cannot be trusted in troops together as ours are, even if there was ground unenclosed for them to graze on, like the common lands in Great Britain.

A nobleman's park is another object never to be seen or expected in a country where people would really be deserving much blame did they retain in their hands for mere amusement ten or twelve miles' circuit of earth, capable to produce two or three thousand pounds a year profit to their families, beside making many tenants rich and happy in the meantime. I will confess, however, that the absence of all these *agrémens* gives a flatness and uniformity to the views which we cannot complain of in England; but when Italians consider the cause, they will have reason to be satisfied with the effect, especially while vegetable nature flourishes in full perfection, while every step crushes out perfume from the trodden herbs, and those in the hedges dispense with delightful liberality a fragrance that enchants one. Hops and pyracanthus cover the sides of every cottage, and the scent of truffles attracts, and the odour of melons gratifies one's nerves when driving among the habitations of fertile Lombardy.

Milan.

We are now cutting hay here for the last time this season, and all the environs smell like spring on this 15th September, 1786. The autumnal tint, however, falls fast upon the trees, which are already rich with a deep yellow hue. A wintry feel upon the atmosphere early in a morning, heavy fogs about noon, and a hollow wind towards the approach of night, make it look like the very last week of October in England, and warn us that summer is going. The same circumstances prompt me, who am about to forsake this her favourite region, to provide furs, flannels, etc., for the passing of those Alps which look so formidable when covered with snow, even at their present distance. Our swallows are calling their clamorous council round me while I write; but the butterflies still flutter about in the middle of the day, and grapes are growing more wholesome, as with us when the mornings begin to be frosty. Our desserts, however, do not remind us of Tuscany; the cherries here are not particularly fine, and the peaches all part from the stone—miserable things! An English gardener would not send them to table. The figs, too, were infinitely finer at Leghorn, and nectarines have I never seen at all.

Well, here is the opera begun again. Some merry wag—Abate Casti, I think—has accommodated and adapted the old story of King Theodore to put in ridicule the present King of Sweden, who is hated of the emperor for some political reasons—I forget what—and he, of course, patronizes the jester. Our honest Lombards, however, take no delight in mimicry, and feel more disgust than pleasure when simplicity is insulted, or distress made more corrosive by the bitterness of a scoffing spirit. I have tried to see whether they would laugh at any oddity in their neighbour's manner, but never could catch any, except perhaps now and then a sly Roman who had a liking for it. 'I see nothing absurd about the man,' says one gentleman; 'everybody may have some peculiarity, and most people have, but such things make me no sport. Let us, when we have a mind to laugh, go and laugh at Punchinello.' From such critics, therefore, the King of Sweden is safe enough, as they have not yet acquired the taste of hunting down royalty, and crowing with infantine malice when possessed of the mean hope that they are able to pinch a noble heart. This old-fashioned country, which detests the sight of suffering majesty, hisses off its theatre a performance calculated to divert them at the expense of a sovereign prince, whose character is clear from blame, and whose personal weaknesses are protected by his birth and merit, while it is to his open, free, and politely generous behaviour alone they owe the knowledge that he has such foibles. Paisiello, therefore, cannot drive it down by his best music, though the poor King of Sweden is a Lutheran, too, and if anything would make them hate him, that would.

One vice, however, sometimes prevents the commission of another, and that same prevailing idea which prompts these prejudiced Romanists to conclude him doomed to lasting torments who dares differ from them, though in points of no real importance, inspires them at the same time with such compassion for his supposed state of predestinated punishment, that they rather incline to defend him from further misery, and kindly forbear to heap ridicule in this world upon a person who is sure to suffer eternal damnation in the other.

But the Spanish grandee, who not only entertained, but astonished us all one night with his conversation at Quirini's Casino at Venice, is arrived here at Milan, and plays upon the violin. He challenged acquaintance with us in the street, half-invited himself to our private concert last night, and did us the honour to perform there with the skill of a professor, the eager desire of a dilettante, and the tediousness of a solitary student; he continued to amaze, delight, and fatigue us for four long hours together. He is a man of prodigious talents, and replete with variety of knowledge. A new dance has been tried at here, too, but was not well received, though it represents the terrible story which, under Madame de Genlis' pen, had such uncommon success among the reading world, and is called 'La sepolta viva'; but as the Duchess Girafalco, whose misfortune it commemorates, is still alive, the pantomime will probably be suppressed; for she has relations at Milan, it seems, and one lady, distinguished for elegance of form and charms of voice and manner, told me yesterday with equal sweetness, spirit and propriety, that though the King of Naples sent his soldiers to free his aunt from that horrible dungeon, where she had been nine years confined, yet, if her miseries were to become the subject of stage representation, she could hardly be pronounced happy, or even at ease.

With these reflections, and many others, excited by gratitude to private friends and general admiration of a country so justly esteemed, we shall soon take our leave of Milan, famed for her truly hospitable disposition—a temper of mind sometimes abused by travellers, perhaps, whose birth and pretensions are seldom or ever inquired into, whilst no people are more careful of keeping their rank inviolate by never conversing on equal terms with a countryman or woman of their own who cannot produce a proper length of ancestry.

I will not leave them, though, without another

word or two about their language, which, though it sounded strangely coarse and broad, to be sure, as we returned home from Florence, Rome, and Venice, I felt sincerely glad to hear again; and have some notion, by their way of pronouncing 'bicchiere,' a word used here to express everything that holds water, that our 'pitcher' was probably derived from it; and the Abate Divecchio, a polite scholar and an uncommonly agreeable companion, seemed to think so too. His knowledge of the English language, joined to the singular power he has over his own elegant Tuscan tongue, made me torment him with a variety of inquiries about these confusing dialects, which leave me at last little chance to understand any, whilst a child is called 'bambino' at Florence, 'putto' at Venice, 'schiatto' at Bergamo, and 'creatura' at Rome; and at Milan they call a wench 'tosa'; an apron is 'grembiule' at Florence, I think, 'traversa' at Venice, 'bigarrol' at Brescia and some other parts of Lombardy, 'senale' at Rome, and at Milan 'scozzà.' A foreigner may well be distracted by varieties so striking; but the turn and idiom differ ten times more still, and I love to hear our Milanese call an oak 'robur' rather than 'quercia' somehow, and tell a lady when dressed in white that she is 'tutta in albedine.'

Verona.

But it is time to leave all this and rejoice in my third arrival at gay, cheerful, charming Verona, whither some sweet leave-taking verses have followed us, written by the facetious Abate Ravasi, a native of Rome, but for many years an inhabitant of Milan. His agreeable sonnet, every line ending with 'tutto,' being upon a subject of general importance, would serve as a better specimen of his abilities than lines dictated only by partial friendship; but I hear that is already circulated about the world, and printed in one of our magazines. To them let him trust his fame; they will pay my just debts.

We have now seen this enchanting spot in spring, summer and autumn, nor could winter's self render it undelightful, while uniting every charm and gratifying every sense. Greek and Roman antiquities salute one at the gates; Gothic remains render each place of worship venerable; Nature, in her holiday dress, decks the environs, and society animates with intellectual fire the amiable inhabitants. Improvisation at this place pleases me far better than it did in Tuscany. Our truly learned Abate Lorenzi astonishes all who hear him by repeating—not singing—a series of admirably just and well-digested thoughts, which he, and he alone, possesses the power of arranging suddenly as if by magic, and methodically as if by study, to rhymes the most melodious and most varied; while the Abbé Bertola, of the university at Pavia, gives one pleasure by the same talent in a manner totally different, singing his unpremeditated strains to the accompaniment of a harpsichord, round which stand a little chorus of friends, who interpolate from time to time two lines of a well-known song, to which he pleasingly adapts his compositions, and goes on gracing the barren subject and adorning it with every possible decoration of wit and every desirable elegance of sentiment. Nothing can surely surpass the happy promptitude of his expression, unless it is the brilliancy of his genius.

But I will not be seduced by the pleasure of praising my sweet friends at Verona to lengthen this chapter with further panegyrics upon a place I leave with the truest tenderness and with the sincerest regret; while the correspondence I hope long to maintain with the charming Contessa Mosconi must compensate all it can for the loss of her agreeable coterie, where my most delightful evenings have been spent; where so many topics of English literature have been discussed; where Lorenzi read Tasso to us of an afternoon, Bertola made verses, and the Cavalier Pindemonte conversed; where the three Graces, as they are called, joined their sweet voices to sing when satiety of pleasure made us change our mode of being happy, and kept one from wishing ever to hear anything else; while Countess Carminati sung Bianchi's duets with the only tenor fit to accompany a voice so touching and a taste so refined. 'Verona! qui te viderit, et non amarit,' says some old writer—I forget who—' protinus amor perditissimo; is credo se ipsum non amat.'* Indeed, I never saw people live so pleasingly together as these do, the women apparently delighting in each other's company, without mean rivalry or envy of those accomplishments which are commonly bestowed by heaven with diversity enough for all to have their share. The world surely affords room for everybody's talents, would everybody that possessed them but think so; and were malice and affectation once completely banished from cultivated society, Verona might be found in many places perhaps; she is now confined, I think, to the sweet state of Venice.

* 'Whoever sees thee without being smitten with extraordinary passion, must, I think, be incapable of loving even himself.'

THE END

EVENTS OF OUR OWN TIME.

A Series of Volumes on the most Important Events of the last Half Century, each containing 300 pages or more, in large 8vo, with Plans, Portraits, or other Illustrations, to be issued at intervals. Price per Volume, $1.75.

THE WAR IN THE CRIMEA. By General Sir EDWARD HAMLEY, K.C.B. With Five Maps and Plans, and Four Portraits on Copper, namely :—

    THE EMPEROR NICHOLAS.   LORD RAGLAN.
    GENERAL TODLEBEN.   COUNCIL OF WAR.

THE INDIAN MUTINY OF 1857. By Colonel MALLESON, C.S.I. With Three Plans, and Four Portraits on Copper, namely :—

    LORD CLYDE.   SIR HENRY LAWRENCE.
    GENERAL HAVELOCK.   SIR JAMES OUTRAM.

ACHIEVEMENTS IN ENGINEERING. By Professor VERNON HARCOURT. With many Illustrations.

THE AFGHAN WAR. By ARCHIBALD FORBES. With several Plans, and Portraits on Copper of

    SIR FRED. ROBERTS.   SIR LOUIS CAVAGNARI.
    SIR GEORGE POLLOCK.   AMEER ABDURRAHMAN.

THE DEVELOPMENT OF NAVIES. By Captain EARDLEY WILMOT, R.N. With many Illustrations.

(In Preparation.)

THE LIBERATION OF ITALY. With Portraits on Copper.

THE REFOUNDING OF THE GERMAN EMPIRE. With Portraits on Copper.

THE EXPLORATION OF AFRICA. With Portraits on Copper.

THE CIVIL WAR IN AMERICA. With Portraits on Copper.

THE OPENING OF JAPAN. With Illustrations.

Other Volumes will follow.

NEW YORK: CHARLES SCRIBNERS' SONS.

LITERARY AND SOCIAL LIFE.

LADY MARY WORTLEY MONTAGU.
By ARTHUR R. ROPES, M.A., Sometime Fellow of King's College, Cambridge. With Nine Portraits after Sir Godfrey Kneller. Cloth extra, $2.50.

MRS. THRALE (afterwards Mrs. PIOZZI).
By L. B. SEELEY, M.A, Sometime Fellow of Trinity College, Cambridge. With Nine Copper Plates after Hogarth, etc. Cloth, $2.50.

FANNY BURNEY AND HER FRIENDS.
By L. B. SEELEY, M.A., Sometime Fellow of Trinity College, Cambridge. With Nine Copper Plates after Gainsborough, etc. Cloth, $2.50.

HORACE WALPOLE AND HIS WORLD.
By L. B. SEELEY, M.A., Sometime Fellow of Trinity College, Cambridge. With Eight Copper Plates after Reynolds, etc. Cloth, $2.50.

GLIMPSES OF ITALIAN SOCIETY IN THE EIGHTEENTH CENTURY.
From the "Journey" of Mrs. PIOZZI. With an Introduction by the Countess MARTINENGO CESARESCO, and several Illustrations. Cloth, $1.75.

NEW YORK: CHARLES SCRIBNERS' SONS.

www.ingramcontent.com/pod-product-compliance
Lightning Source LLC
Chambersburg PA
CBHW020227240426
43672CB00006B/445